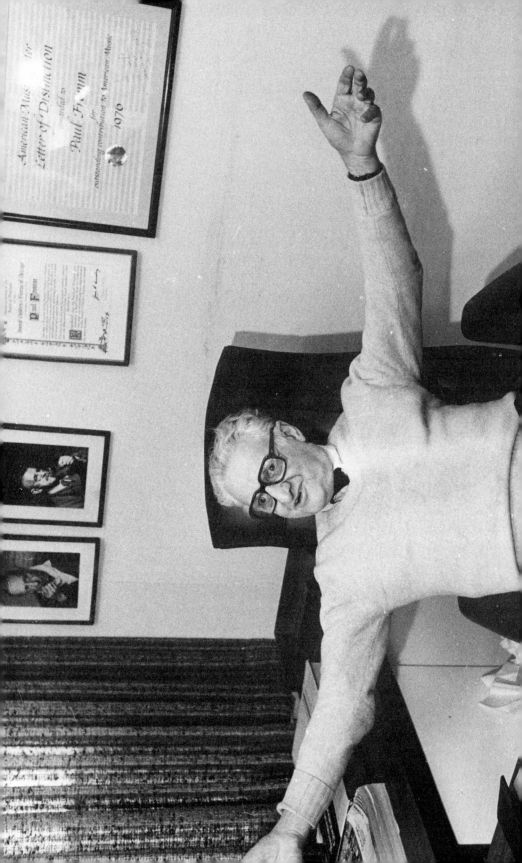

THE FROMM MUSIC FOUNDATION 1952-1987

A LIFE FOR NEW MUSIC

SELECTED PAPERS OF PAUL FROMM

. . . .

Edited by
David Gable and Christoph Wolff

Department of Music · Harvard University
Distributed by Harvard University Press
Cambridge, Massachusetts · 1988

Library of Congress Cataloging-in-Publication Data

Fromm, Paul, 1906-1987.
A life for new music.

At head of title: The Fromm Music Foundation, 1952-1987.

1. Music—20th century—History and criticism.
2. Music and society. 3. Fromm, Paul, 1906-1987.
I. Gable, David, 1955- . II. Wolff, Christoph.
III. Babbitt, Milton, 1916- . IV. Fromm Music Foundation.
V. Title.

ML60.F86   1988   780'.973   88-34718
ISBN 0-674-53088-8

Contents

. . . .

Preface

"**A** Life for New Music"—no other phrase could capture more appropriately and meaningfully the deep enthusiasm, inspiring dedication, vigorous efforts, and generous benefactions that have marked Paul Fromm's lifelong commitment to the cause of contemporary music. Last year the sad news of his death on July 4, 1987, quickly went around the globe and reached the wider new music community that he had helped to enlarge and inspire. We mourned the loss of a close friend—to some of us a personal, to all of us a congenial one. We remember an extraordinary man, we celebrate his life, we thank him. How can we best pay a memorial tribute to him?

The most important and lasting memorial will be the enduring operation of the Fromm Music Foundation, which Paul Fromm established in 1952 with the unique, unprecedented, and exclusive aim of helping create new musical works and to bring about, in his own words, "a meaningful interaction among composers, performers, and audiences." The Fromm Music Foundation at Harvard will continue to follow a clearly marked path in the spirit of its founder and in the hope of emulating his imaginative vision in perpetuity. In this way Paul Fromm, always a profoundly forward-looking man, will continue to contribute to the shaping of the music of the future.

The present volume is meant to be a documentary memorial. At its core is a selection of Paul Fromm's writings, most of them originally presented as talks that indicate very clearly his personal concerns and views. The list of commissioned compositions impressively reflects the specific results as well as the unique impact on the contemporary music scene that the Fromm Music Foundation has brought about over the period of thirty-five years under Paul Fromm's energetic, far-sighted, unorthodox, and non-parochial direction. The tributes by five of Paul Fromm's closest composer friends, Milton Babbitt, Luciano Berio, Pierre Boulez, Elliott Carter, and Ralph Shapey, demonstrate in a representative way his "Renaissance" concept of patronage as well as his desire and ability to foster faithful and productive interrelationships.

On behalf of the Directors of the Fromm Music Foundation I wish to thank Dr. Erika Fromm, Paul's widow, and Cecile Edelstein, his long-time secretary, for their help in the preparation of this volume. David Gable, who served Paul Fromm during his last years as assistant on Foundation matters, deserves special thanks for his devoted and expert editorial work.

Christoph Wolff
Harvard University
May, 1988

. . . .

Paul Fromm in American Musical Life[1]

With the death of Paul Fromm on 4 July, 1987, contemporary American music lost its premiere patron. It may be difficult for a European to appreciate how important this one man could be for contemporary American music, but no American composer can be unaware of Fromm's significance, for virtually no American composer can have escaped being Fromm's beneficiary, if only indirectly. There are simply more avenues open to a European composer for performance, subsidy, patronage, and publication than for even the most respected, established, American composer. "This country!" as Elliott Carter once lamented:

> We're so large, culture is so diffused. New music has never burst into flame. There's never been an intensive effort to put it across, not since Koussevitzky and Stokowski. There are wonderful soloists devoted to playing a lot to small audiences for little pay, but the long effort to project contemporary music publicly has not succeeded.[2]

Where a latter-day Koussevitzky or Stokowski may have been lacking, Paul Fromm seized a unique opportunity to step into the breach on behalf of composers within America's peculiar cultural situation. Fromm's sustained experiment in music patronage unfolded within a modern bourgeois democracy largely lacking the traditions of aristocratic, church, and state patronage that have characterized the history of European art music. The papers of Paul Fromm collected for this volume constitute a document of that experiment.

Born in Kitzingen, Germany, in 1906, a fifth-generation member of a family of vintners, Fromm was early an amateur of music. Given piano lessons as a child, he delighted in playing the piano, four hands, repertoire and transcriptions of the standard repertoire with his brother Herbert, who later pursued a career as a composer. Fromm became aware of contemporary music in the early 1920s when he first heard a performance of Stravinsky's *Rite of Spring:* "It made a twentieth century man of me." From 1921 to 1926 he attended concerts of contemporary music in Germany's Black Forest at the Donaueschingen Festival, where much of the advanced music of the period could be heard.

---

1. A version of this Introduction is forthcoming in *The Contemporary Music Review.*
2. Schwartz, Lloyd, "Elliott Carter and the conflict of chaos and order," *Harvard Magazine*, 86/2 (December 1983), p. 60.

Until quite late in his life, Fromm preferred to listen to new music with score in hand, although he once sardonically remarked of an especially simplistic score that its merit was immediately cast into doubt by his ability to read it. In his seventy-ninth year, Fromm even took up the study of harmony, although an unbelievably demanding if self-imposed schedule prevented him from pursuing too many of the exercises in Roger Sessions's *Harmonic Practice.*

Fromm first hoped to become a patron of music in Germany; he was planning the establishment of a music foundation in his native land when he was forced to flee the Nazi pogroms in 1938. Settling in Chicago, he went into business as a wine importer, co-founding the Geeting and Fromm Corporation in 1939, founding the Great Lakes Wine Company in 1943.[3] In 1944 he became a naturalized citizen of the United States. In 1952 he established the Fromm Music Foundation, which was incorporated in the state of Illinois. In 1972, the Foundation moved to Harvard University, although Fromm continued to conduct most of its business out of his office at Great Lakes Wine Company in the warehouse district of Chicago. Fromm delighted in shocking visitors who wished to see the Foundation offices by pointing to a bank of filing cabinets.

Fromm's modesty, humanity, and generosity are abundantly evident in a statement he made to composer Arthur Berger in 1959. Fromm felt that he had:

> become too prosperous. I can now buy happiness for others. The employer can now serve his employees by giving them spiritual leadership in return for their service. Otherwise we shall succumb in the next twenty-five years to a new lonesomeness, a spiritual bankruptcy. I don't want to be thanked for what I do. Nothing embarrasses me more. The composer is the one who deserves *our* thanks. I despise the relationship between Santa Claus and deserving child. This is *not* social work. Ours is not an aid society. I fulfill my obligations to social work by running a therapeutic nursing service for mentally disturbed children.[4]

The Foundation's philanthropic services to composers began quietly and without fanfare. In the beginning, Fromm privately distributed commissions to deserving composers, frequently paying for already completed but unremunerated work. His underground reputation was soon well established.

An enduring and remarkable aspect of the Foundation has been its personal and unbureaucratic nature. This is due in large measure to the close ties that Paul Fromm kept to the Foundation and to all of its operations. While the Foundation began with a Board of Directors, Fromm soon disbanded this Board, retaining only the violinist-conductor Alexander Schneider as an Associate Director. Fromm was then free to seek advice of Aaron Copland or Gunther Schuller at Tanglewood, for example, or of Roger Sessions or Milton Babbitt at Princeton University, or of Ralph Shapey or Robert P. Morgan in Chicago. Thus Babbitt recommended that Fromm commission Shapey,

3. Geeting & Fromm was founded on July 29, 1939, for retail wine sales and sold by Fromm in 1979. Great Lakes Wine Company, founded August 21, 1943, and sold in 1981, existed for the wholesale wine trade.

4. Berger, Arthur, "What Mozart Didn't Have: The Story of the Fromm Music Foundation," *High Fidelity,* IX/2 (1959), p. 43.

Copland that Fromm commission Luciano Berio, and so forth. (Fromm first commissioned both Berio and Shapey in 1960.) A healthy flexibility has characterized the Foundation since its inception.

While the vast majority of composers Fromm has commissioned have been Americans, this commission for Berio is symptomatic of Fromm's undogmatic flexibility. When Berio first met Fromm at Tanglewood in 1960, he had never received a commission. Already the author of a considerable body of extremely accomplished works, Berio received his first commission from the Fromm Foundation. This resulted in the composition of *Circles,* one of his most widely known pieces. Berio is probably the European composer to whom Fromm was closest, and, in 1987, Fromm commissioned Berio a second time, to write a work for voice, viola, and digital processor to be realized at the new *Tempo Reale* studio in Florence that Berio heads.

When Berio presented the English translation of a book of his interviews to Fromm in 1985, Fromm replied to Berio with warmth and sensitivity:

> The material is as grippingly presented as it is intrinsically interesting. The whole is so absorbing that it is difficult to know what to single out: the interesting glimpses of life in pre-War Italy afforded by anecdotes of your childhood, your aperçus of composers from Monteverdi to Boulez to Puccini, your insights into the inner workings of IRCAM, or your discussions of your own works.

> There is one constant and refreshing feature of your book that illustrates a difference between European and American composers. You are concerned with what might be called the sociology of listening, although in a personally committed way. Your awareness of the varieties of meaning that a variety of musics might potentially hold for a variety of listeners is constantly to the fore in your book. This is explicit when you are talking about, for example, Adorno (your critique of Adorno is one of the acute things in the book), the interest of young people in music, or your television series, "There's music and music." But this consciousness on your part is evident even when it is not the explicit topic, because it underlies and colors all of your thinking. Is it simply that a European composer takes it for granted that music is an integral part of life and society?[5]

Fromm here touched on a theme that reappeared as a refrain throughout his life: the integration of contemporary music and the musical life of his adopted country. All of the Foundation's activities were aimed at this utopian goal. The Foundation's activities themselves are not easily summarized, as Fromm has variously attacked the problems of contemporary music as the situation merited, but he best summarized his own philosophy in 1959 at a Princeton University seminar:

> The Seminar In Advanced Musical Studies grew out of the same concern with the realities and necessities of American musical life that has motivated all the activities of the Fromm Music Foundation. Our efforts have never been intended to be patronage in the old sense of comprehensive

5. Fromm, Paul, unpublished letter to Luciano Berio of 4 September 1985.

support of a segment of musical activity or a group of artists, but rather a series of stimulants that should focus attention, by their example, upon the most promising aspects of creative activity.[6]

The Foundation's commissioning program is absolutely central to its activities. Fromm has commissioned nearly two hundred works from more than one hundred and fifty composers, but Fromm has not been content merely to dispense commissions. In his efforts to integrate contemporary music within the mainstream of musical life, the Foundation has also funded the first performances of virtually all of these works. Further, Fromm has striven to place commissioned works in concert programs all over the country so that new works have not disappeared, as so often happens, after the first performance.

The Foundation's multifarious activities have included the sponsorship of hundreds of concerts, including such festivals as the Festival of Contemporary Arts at the University of Illinois (Urbana) in 1957 and the first Roger Sessions Festival, which took place at Northwestern University in 1961 and included performances of the composer's opera *The Trial of Lucullus,* as well as of chamber and orchestral works. There have also been recordings: in the 1950s and '60s of works by Elliott Carter, Luigi Dallapiccola, Lukas Foss, Leon Kirchner, Ernst Krenek, and Ben Weber on the Epic label; since 1987 on New World Records, beginning with a recording of Shapey's works. Fromm also sponsored a series of radio programs on station WFMT in Chicago in the early 1960s in which composers presented their own music or that of early twentieth-century masters.

A long-standing relationship between the Berkshire Music Center at Tanglewood, the summer home of the Boston Symphony Orchestra, and the Fromm Foundation began in 1956. Fromm recalled the origins of the relationship:

> One of the serious problems in our musical culture has been the frustrating isolation of young composers and performers from each other, which is intensified by the often unsympathetic attitude of performers towards the music of our time. Although this situation has been abundantly recognized, most attempts at alleviation have been diffuse and sporadic. We therefore determined to begin our own efforts in this direction with a concentrated experiment.[7]

In 1956, Aaron Copland,[8] head of the Composition Department at the Berkshire Music Center since 1940, accepted Fromm's invitation to head this project, which ultimately embraced three programs: a commissioning program, the Fromm Fellowship Players, and, from 1964, an annual Tanglewood Festival of Contemporary music. The commissioning program sponsored young composers who were also invited to be on hand for a period of two weeks to supervise rehearsals of new work. The Fromm Fellowship Players enabled young performers to study and perform new music, including that of the commissioned composers. These two programs functioned from 1956 to 1984.

6. Fromm, Paul, "The Princeton Seminar—Its Purpose and Promise," *The Musical Quarterly,* XLVI/2 (1960), p. 155.
7. *Ibid.*
8. Aaron Copland, who dedicated his book *The New Music: 1900-1960* (New York, 1968) to Paul Fromm, was invited to contribute his reminiscences to this volume, but failing health prevented him from doing so.

The Festival itself, which came to be known as "Fromm Week," was an annual series of chamber and orchestral performances of contemporary music by members of the Boston Symphony. In 1964, Erich Leinsdorf, Music Director of the Boston Symphony Orchestra from 1962 to 1969, assumed responsibility for the Boston Symphony's summer activities at the Berkshire Music Center. The relationship between the Boston Symphony and the Foundation was particularly close during Leinsdorf's tenure, as Leinsdorf was a warm supporter of new music. That same year, Gunther Schuller assumed direction of contemporary music activities at the Berkshire Music Center. Schuller directed contemporary music activities there from 1964 to 1984, becoming a trusted advisor to Paul Fromm. Fromm, Leinsdorf, and Schuller planned the first Tanglewood Festival of Contemporary Music. There would be annual "Fromm Weeks" at Tanglewood from 1964 to 1983.

One of the most distinguished programs ever funded by The Fromm Foundation took place on January 4, 1959, at New York's Town Hall, where Robert Craft conducted the American premieres of Alban Berg's already forty-six-year-old *Altenberg Lieder* and Stravinsky's new *Threni* (1958). *Threni*, thus rehearsed by Craft, was taken into the CBS recording studios for a composer-led recording to be made for Columbia records. Stravinsky had met Fromm the previous year. "I want to know you," Stravinsky said to Fromm, "because contemporary music has many friends but only a few lovers."[9] Relations remained cordial after this initial contact and Fromm received Stravinsky's fleeting input on more than one occasion. On Stravinsky's eightieth birthday in 1962, Fromm presented the composer with four twenty-year-old bottles of whiskey.

In September of 1961, a concert for the Eighth Congress of the International Musicological Society was the occasion for the premieres of two new works that had been commissioned by the Fromm Foundation: Milton Babbitt's *Vision and Prayer* and Elliott Carter's *Double Concerto*. Babbitt's work was written for the extraordinary soprano Bethany Beardslee, who has been so closely identified with Babbitt's music, and for tape, so its performance did not pose the same rehearsal problems that Carter's work did. Charles Rosen, the pianist for Carter's *Concerto*, recalls the circumstances surrounding the Carter premiere:

> In the summer of 1961, I received the last pages of the Double Concerto in Paris a few days before flying to New York for the first rehearsal. It is not only eighteenth-century musicians, waiting for Mozart to blot the wet ink on the score, who have had to learn a new work at the last moment . . . .The final section or coda contained the most complicated rhythmic passage I had ever been asked to play . . . I had not yet succeeded in persuading my left hand to ignore what my right hand was doing when I had to leave for New York and one of New York's late-summer heat waves. Rehearsals took place during a ten-day period in which the weather frustrated a sane and cool approach to a difficult new work. The luxury of ten days of rehearsal was due to the generosity of Paul Fromm, who commissioned the work and allowed the composer his choice of performers.

9. Nelson, Boris, "Paul Fromm, Contemporary Music's Friend and Lover," *Toledo Blade* (2 August, 1987), Section E, p. 3.

The small chamber orchestra was made up of the best of New York's free-lance players with a considerable awareness of contemporary style.[10]

The harpsichordist was Ralph Kirkpatrick, the conductor Gustave Meier. Despite its difficulties, the *Double Concerto* has gone on to receive hundreds of performances around the world and three recordings. Indeed, Fromm often referred to the *Double Concerto* as the Foundation's *Firebird.*

In 1959 and 1960, the Fromm Foundation and Princeton University jointly sponsored two Seminars in Advanced Musical Studies that were intended to benefit young composers. Inspired in part by the summer courses at Darmstadt, these seminars were essentially the brainchild of Fromm and Roger Sessions. In 1959, twenty-five young composers studied with a distinguished faculty that included Sessions, Milton Babbitt, Edward T. Cone, Robert Craft, and Ernst Krenek. Elliott Carter, Aaron Copland, and Edgar Varèse also lectured, while Stravinsky appeared briefly to speak with the participants. The second seminar, with Babbitt, Carter and Sessions again present, featured eleven Fromm Fellowship Players; the absence of available performers within such a workshop situation had been acutely felt the previous year. The Players were on hand to realize compositions in progress or excerpts from scores under discussion. The papers presented at the first seminar were subsequently published both in *The Musical Quarterly* and as a book entitled *Problems of New Music.*[11]

These seminars also led to the birth of a new periodical, as Paul Fromm explains:

> [T]he very success of these seminars served to reveal their limitations, for it became increasingly apparent during the two summer sessions that such intensive interchange was needed by all composers as a continuous and permanent aspect of their professional lives. We realized, in fact, that the absence of such continuous orientation is partially responsible for the uncertain position of the American composer . . .
>
> To overcome the limited range of even so promising an undertaking as the Princeton Seminars, we decided to establish . . . a forum of considerably broader scope.[12]

In the late 1950s and early '60s, many composers felt that such a forum for discussion of contemporary music was needed. Stravinsky summed up this growing sentiment:

> One solution to the question of what to do with Brother Criticus would be for composers to publish their own review . . . the important thing is that it should be a composer's—i.e., a professional—review. The chief obstacle to an enterprise of this sort is not money, of course, but the editorial time required of the composers, and the probable disinclination of the composers themselves to write . . . Several age groups must be represented, first of all, and their consequent . . . points of view. Who is qualified to

10. Rosen, Charles, "One Easy Piece," *The New York Review of Books,* XX/2 (1973), p. 26; reprinted in Rosen, Charles, *The Musical Language of Elliott Carter,* Washington, D.C., 1984, pp. 23-34.

11. *The Musical Quarterly,* XLVI/2 (1960); reprinted as Paul Henry Lang, editor, *Problems of Modern Music,* New York, 1962.

12. Fromm, Paul, "Young Composers: Perspective and Prospect," *Perspectives of New Music,* I/1 (1962), p. 2.

write? Indeed, who among composers can write? The elder statesmen, people like Virgil Thomson, Roberto Gerhard, Ernst Krenek, Roger Sessions, are the most articulate and the strictest in their integrity of words. In the next-to-senior group, the first names to occur to me are Milton Babbitt, Elliott Carter, George Perle, Arthur Berger, and, of the middle-aged group, Boulez. I am not familiar enough with the work of such talked-about younger composers as Peter Maxwell Davies, Dieter Schönbach, Giacomo Manzoni to be qualified to recommend any of them, but I know that the point of view of their generation should be voiced.[13]

Babbitt, Carter, and Sessions were among the many American composers who had expressed similar sentiments to Paul Fromm. Sensitive to this perceived lacuna, Fromm sponsored a new journal that was to be published by Princeton University Press. *Perspectives of New Music* saw the light of day in 1962. The editors of the journal were composers Arthur Berger and Benjamin Boretz.[14] Fromm, who maintained close ties with members of the journal's editorial board, was "anything but an inactive sponsor," as Boretz recalls.[15]

The first two issues of *Perspectives* included contributions by composers Babbitt, Boulez, Carter, Foss, Imbrie, Krenek, Schuller, Stravinsky, Stockhausen, Westergaard, and Wuorinen as well as other articles by critics Edward Cone, Charles Rosen, and Michael Steinberg and theorists Allen Forte and David Lewin. The breadth of scope that this partial list of contributors betokens fit the editorial prescriptions envisioned by the new journal's patron. Several important anthologies have been culled from *Perspectives* and published in book form.[16]

Unfortunately, the history of the relationship between the Fromm Foundation and the brave new journal did not prove to be a happy one. After the first issues, Fromm was disturbed that an exclusive viewpoint came to dominate the journal. However intrinsically valuable the kinds of analytic approaches that came to typify it may be, *Perspectives* did become in essence a highly specialized theory journal for contemporary music. For a decade, Fromm and certain members of the advisory board attempted to broaden the journal's scope, and when the editorial board of the journal refused to return to the original conception, Fromm withdrew his funding in 1972.

Happier by far have been Fromm's relations with Ralph Shapey and the Contemporary Chamber Players of the University of Chicago. Shapey's intransigence had militated against the easy acceptance of his music, but Fromm became one of Shapey's most persuasive advocates. Fromm commissioned Shapey no less than three times. Further, in the mid-1960s, Fromm funded a number of concerts of the Contemporary

13. Stravinsky, Igor and Robert Craft, *Expositions and Developments*, New York, 1962, p. 171.
14. Berger and Boretz were editors of the semi-annual *Perspectives of New Music* for the first three issues. Boretz was sole editor of the next four issues. Edward T. Cone joined Boretz as editor in 1966 with volume 4, number 2.
15. Berger, Arthur and Benjamin Boretz, "A Conversation about Perspectives," *Perspectives of New Music*, XXV/1,2 (1987), p. 600.
16. Boretz, Benjamin and Edward T. Cone, editors, *Perspectives on Schoenberg and Stravinsky*, Princeton, 1968; *Perspectives on American Composers*, New York, 1972; *Perspectives on Contemporary Music Theory*, New York, 1972; *Perspectives on Notation and Performance*, New York, 1972.

Chamber Players, which Shapey had founded in 1964. By 1967, an annual Fromm concert had become established within the Contemporary Chamber Players' season. A work newly commissioned by the Foundation has appeared on virtually every Contemporary Chamber Players Fromm Concert since. This annual event will continue with an endowment left to the ensemble by Shapey's intimate friend and benefactor.

In 1972, the Foundation celebrated its twentieth anniversary. Bruno Maderna, Gunther Schuller, Roger Sessions, and Charles Wuorinen were all commissioned to mark the occasion. Shapey conducted the premiere of the Sessions *Concertino* in Chicago. Maderna and Schuller conducted the premieres of their own works, *Giardino Religioso* and *Music for Chamber Ensemble*, at Tanglewood, where Michael Tilson Thomas led the premiere of Wuorinen's *Concerto for Amplified Violin*. With the exception of the Wuorinen, these works were all subsequently recorded.

1972 also marked the Foundation's relocation to Harvard University. Fromm explained the move:

> If . . . our efforts on behalf of contemporary music were vital, our concern must now be to ensure that they remain vital. Human institutions stand ever in need of renewal and revitalization, and the time has come to end the era in which the Fromm Music Foundation was simply an extension of myself. We must move on to a new era in which the Foundation must be able to exist independently of any one individual.[17]

Henceforth the Foundation would be governed by a Board of Directors consisting of Fromm, the Chairman of the Department of Music at Harvard University, and an established American composer. Gunther Schuller, with whom Fromm had collaborated so successfully at Tanglewood, was the first composer appointed.

For the celebrations of the Bicentennial of the United States in 1976, the Fromm Foundation collaborated with the New York Philharmonic and the Juilliard School of Music on a large-scale festival of contemporary American music that was in some ways a culmination of Foundation activities. The time was ripe for such a venture above all because Pierre Boulez was then Music Director of the New York Philharmonic, although the festival seems to have received initial impetus from Fromm. The festival planners decided, in Fromm's words, that "rather than invite composers to write music to celebrate the independence of the Republic, the Republic might celebrate the independence achieved by music in America in the last forty years."[18] Fromm noted that the United States had come a long way since the the day when Richard Wagner had been commissioned to write a march to commemorate the American Centennial. On March 5, 1976, Boulez led the New York Philharmonic in a program of works by Sessions, Jacob Druckman, and Maderna opening an eight-day festival featuring chamber and orchestral works and a number of first performances.

17. Fromm, Paul, *The Fromm Music Foundation: Past, Present, and Future* (privately published brochure), Chicago, 1972; printed below, p. 71-73.
18. Fromm, Paul, "Towards a Bicentennial Celebration of Music in America: An Introductory Note," *Celebration of Contemporary Music* (program book to New York Philharmonic festival of the same name), New York, 1976.

By 1983, Fromm had grown distressed with what he perceived to be the growing insularity of the programming at the annual "Fromm Week" at Tanglewood. Fromm and Schuller, who was still on the Foundation's Board and head of the composition department at Tanglewood, were unable to reach an amicable agreement concerning contemporary music programming there. Schuller resigned from the Foundation's Board of Directors and the Foundation substantially reduced its support at Tanglewood. Fromm's motivations were the same in this instance as in the unfortunate episode of the journal *Perspectives of New Music;* Fromm found there to be insufficient breadth of viewpoint represented and set about redressing the balance. An internal restructuring of the Foundation ensued.

Fromm invited Earle Brown to replace Schuller on the Board of Directors, selecting him for the breadth of his interests within the contemporary field. Fromm deliberately selected a composer who was sympathetic to a broad range of viewpoints and tolerant of divergent aesthetic stances. For similar reasons, nine regional advisors were chosen to represent divergent geographical as well as musical interests. The annual "Fromm Week" of contemporary music relocated to the Aspen Festival in 1985. The programming there has been aggressively heterogeneous; the "new pluralism" has been well represented in all of its bewildering variety.

1985 also saw the inauguration of The Fromm Foundation Visiting Professorship at Harvard University. Peter Maxwell Davies was the first Visiting Professor and was in residence at Harvard for a full term. In 1988, the Visiting Professor was Milton Babbitt. The Professorship will be held every third year.

During the thirty-five years that Paul Fromm directed his Foundation's activities, he acquired friendships with composers too numerous to mention, but among these many friends, Fromm was probably closest to four: Milton Babbitt, Elliott Carter, Ralph Shapey and his collaborator of many years, Gunther Schuller. Fromm regularly turned to Babbitt for advice, particularly to solicit recommendations of promising young composers. Fromm twice commissioned Babbitt, most recently commissioning *Canonical Forms* for pianist Robert Taub in 1983. Fromm, who admired Babbitt's enduring fidelity to exacting ideals, remarked of Babbitt's *Piano Concerto* shortly after its premiere in 1986 that it contained more music than another composer would pour into half a dozen concerti.

Fromm enjoyed a particularly warm relationship with Carter, with whose each new work he was genuinely eager to become familiar. There is a particularly voluminous correspondence between them, Carter's letters to Fromm constituting a virtual diary of his compositional career and musical experiences here and in Europe.

A discussion of Fromm's philanthropy outside of the music world is beyond the scope of this essay. Suffice it to say that Fromm was a citizen who took his social responsibilities seriously. This can be gauged in part by his commissioning policies. Careful to avoid the endemic sexism of the music world where the woman composer is a relatively recent social phenomenon, Fromm made a point of commissioning the most gifted women composers of today; but he also foresaw a time when to do so will not be to make a special point, when the expression "woman composer" with its implicit special pleading will have fallen into desuetude:

> Our responsibility to women composers of the present is very different
> from our responsibility to those of the past. We ought not to segregate

the music of women in ghetto concerts but to play it on regular programs . . . I don't think we do women composers of today a service by
offering them a handicap as if they were golfers who hit way over par.
To do so is to continue to patronize them. We need to evaluate contemporary women composers by the same standards that apply to male composers.[19]

This quotation is from the last public address that Fromm ever gave, "Creative
Women in Music: A Historical Perspective," which he delivered at Tulane University
in 1986. As the activities of the Fromm Foundation became well known, Fromm was
frequently invited to speak. Often the resultant talks were occasional pieces or ephemeral
introductions, but when, as in this instance, Fromm was allotted sufficient time for
inquiries of more ambitious scope, the results were often substantial. It is from these
more substantial talks that the current selection of papers was made.

The selection of papers for this volume spans the period from 1966 to 1986, but
this statistic is misleading. Most of the papers selected date from 1974 to 1986, in
part because the majority of Fromm's longer papers date from this period. Moreover,
he sometimes recycled portions of older material in his later papers. At the same time,
Fromm's ideas evolved so that the later papers are more fully developed. To cite one
example, the 1985 Aspen address "Music Criticism in the Pluralistic Eighties," which
is printed below, both borrows from and is superior to the 1969 Tanglewood address,
"Critical Views on Music Criticism,"[20] which we have elected not to include.

In the presentation of the papers selected, there is a progression from the more general
to the more narrowly focused. Nevertheless, even such potentially dry topics as "A
Role for American Music Libraries" and "The Role of Symphony Boards" provoked
from Fromm more generally applicable remarks than these titles might suggest. From
unexpected angles this selection of articles collectively exposes both Fromm's enduring preoccupation with the incorporation of contemporary music into American musical
life and his fertile and imaginative responses to the problems encountered on the path
to this goal. It is not only the informed patron and pragmatic utopian who emerges
here, but the true amateur in the deepest sense of the word.

The figure of the patron is a shadowy intermediary in the history of the arts; Paul
Fromm, whose life is inextricably interwoven within the history of recent musical creation, modestly claimed that he would at most be a footnote in music history. Nevertheless, he was in so many ways the enabling agent for some of the most remarkable music
written during his lifetime. Fromm's example demonstrated what could be accomplished
with relatively modest means on behalf of a valuable but fragile human enterprise
through the industry and imagination of one man.

David Gable

---

19. Fromm, Paul, "Creative Women in Music: A Historical Perspective" (unpublished address presented
on 3 February 1986 at Tulane University in New Orleans); printed below, p. 42-51.
20. Fromm, Paul, "Critical Views on Music Criticism," unpublished paper delivered on 12 August 1969
at the Berkshire Music Center, Tanglewood.

MEMORIAL TRIBUTES

Paul Fromm:
A Memoir

My life with the Fromm Foundation began with a whimper in 1952, when I received a discreetly engraved, impersonal invitation to submit my music for perusal and evaluation by an identified board of judges whose approval would result in publication and/or recording and/or deposit in the Newberry Library. Since my perusal of the names of the board members strongly suggested that my music would meet the fate it already had suffered many times at the hands, or eyes, or (just possibly) ears of the Guggenheim Foundation Committee, and the glamorous participating publisher and recording company were surely out of my league of composers, I decided that the better part of discretion was not to respond to the invitation. But a few weeks later I received a note tartly reminding me that I had not responded to the generous invitation, so I did, with a brief message explaining my lack of desire to engage in a surely demeaning and probably futile importunity. This time the foundation failed to respond.

All was quiet for five years. Then, in the summer of 1957, I joined the composition faculty of the Berkshire Music Center, Tanglewood, where I lived at Chef Karl's, mainly a fine, honest restaurant (and, therefore, long since gone) owned by a Swiss couple, which provided lodgings in a few rooms on the floor above the restaurant. On one of my first nights (perhaps the very first) there, I emerged from my room on my way down to dinner when a large figure emerged from another room and addressed me by name. Perhaps because of his accent, I momentarily thought that I finally was meeting Chef Karl himself, but the next few words from the figure were: "I am Paul Fromm. I remember your letter and I came to agree with it. I fired my board." (Could it be, I wondered, that honesty—or, at least, candor— ultimately paid? Apparently it did, at least for many memorable years.) At dinner that evening Paul revealed that he not only had jettisoned the board, but severed his connections with the publisher and recording company, whose true devotion to contemporary American music he had come to suspect. So, the first—and, to this day the sole—foundation devoted to the contemporary, mainly American, composer had undergone its first change of heart, and I was to be one of the beneficiaries of the change.

So long and candidly did we talk that first evening that I felt free, finally, to ask Paul why he had decided to concern himself with the American composer, and his reply was that he had wished, as soon as he was able, to express concretely his gratitude to this country for having provided him with a new homeland; so he decided to discover those most needy and worthy cases, and concluded that they were American composers and emotionally disturbed children. Such was the unity of his vision. And now he had determined further that the solution for the American composer was not in printed scores piled in warehouses, or undistributed discs, or library deposits, but in appropriately prepared representations of his music in performance. And that music with which his board had been least concerned—the most demanding, difficult, intricate music—had been most sinned against in that and other respects: in those long, largely unremunerated months of creation, the greater difficulties and expenses of the preparation of materials, and the inadequate number of rehearsals, resulting necessarily in unsatisfactory performances. Add to these obstacles the resistance, even hostility, on the part of the performers, conductors, and entrepreneurs, and Paul regretted only that he was unable to assist at all of these stages. But he was determined to secure composers the kind of apposite performance The Society for Private Performance had promised in its time, and always to begin with the composer, not (as later did the Ford and Rockefeller Foundations and—so often—the NEA) with the performer. He had concluded that allowing the performer to decide what should and could be composed and performed was closely comparable with permitting the printer to decide what books could be written and published. Music, he had come to believe, was not a "performing art" but a creative art.

To this end, that summer of 1957 there was brought to Tanglewood the Fromm Fellowship Players, a group of young professional performers who played the works of the composer students, collaborated in the public lectures of the members of the composition faculty, and met once or twice a week with all the composers for every imaginable form of collegial symbiosis. The string quartet that emerged from these players called itself the Lenox.

At the Princeton Seminars in Advanced Musical Studies in 1959 and 1960, subsidized by the Fromm Foundation, the lectures and seminars were augmented by, embellished by concerts, often extraordinary concerts. The Seminar brought Paul Jacobs back from Europe; Richard Goode, a teenager, played an unforgettable Schoenberg *Phantasy* with Felix Galimir, not a teenager. But, still, the central concern was the composer. Paul Fromm wrote in the first issue of the then Fromm Foundation's *Perspectives of New Music* in 1962: "We attempted to come to grips with the problems of the young composer at the very moment he is ready to make his own contribution to his art. . . . In the light of the intellectual and artistic integrity and vigor shown by our young composers at Princeton and Tanglewood, I am hopeful that our faith in the possibility of restoring the composer to his proper and essential place at the center of musical life will be vindicated."

In the summer of 1964, after my labors at Darmstadt, I met Paul in Frankfurt. It was his second trip to Germany since his exodus. On his first, he and his wife Erika had brought their American-born daughter Joan to visit her "roots." On this trip he was alone on business, and for the days we were together he, with characteristic generosity, was pleased to introduce me to places and wines, to convince the custodian of the new Frankfurt opera house to take the "professor" on the grand tour. When the limping custodian discovered that Paul had left that part of the world on a rather revealing date, he immediately assured us that he had been injured in a street battle with the Nazis, for he had been a socialist; Paul whispered to me: "Now, they were all socialists."

4

These were only too manifestly a psychologically complex few days for Paul, and during them he told me, as he never had before, the remarkable saga of his having arrived in the United States in 1938, the scion of many generations of distinguished vintners, to spend his first year in Chicago climbing the stairs of office buildings peddling bad wine with fake labels as supplied and commanded by Chicago gangsters. Within a year he founded his own business, with good wine with genuine labels, and soon thereafter was consulted by the United States government on the restoration of the German vineyards. His only regret was that he ever had been persuaded to go to Chicago, rather than advised to stay in New York, since he was certain he would have made much more money in New York, and that would have meant much more money for the Foundation, since (as Arthur Berger revealed in an article in 1959) such money was not the interest from an endowment, but, rather, that each year Paul determined what part of his business's profits the family would need to support its modest lifestyle, what part the business would need, and the remainder was what the Foundation spent.

Since the days of Princeton and Tanglewood, the Fromm Foundation's perspectives have shifted with musical times and tides; the style and ideology of Paul's articles and speeches have changed often, sometimes abruptly. He was too worldly to be affected by journalism's incorrigible caprices or its blandishments, but he was just enough a man of this world to be aware of and occasionally to succumb to its ubiquitous pressures, particularly when Foundation decisions depended upon "Whom do you trust?" But while the mammoth foundations played touch and go, on-again off-again with contemporary music, Paul persisted in his self-imposed support.

Whether he cared or not, I cared very much that Paul received even less his due than did the composers whose fates so concerned him. It reflects far less on the status of Paul than on the state of music among the putative arts that the American Academy-Institute of Arts and Letters never bestowed upon him the Award for Distinguished Service to the Arts, while so honoring a politician who could scarcely wait for his political party to attain power so that he could install his minimally qualified college classmate as chairman of the National Endowment for the Arts, or a society lady whose inherited wealth provided occasional rewards for socially and historically certified institutions.

We shall miss profoundly the many pleasures of Paul's many presences, and while he can rest assured that his Foundation will continue in his spirit (and there never was a letter), we can be sadly certain that just as he was the first of his kind, he very likely was the last and—therefore—the only of his kind.

Milton Babbitt
December 31, 1987

Paul

Paul was a tree. A solitary tree. And a friendly one: an oak, perhaps, an olive tree, a cypress—strong and gentle, with deep intricate roots, its branches full of gifts. Paul had invented his own way to love music: practical and idealistic, aware and emotional. His love for music was made of the same ingredients that endow with meaning any form of creativity. Paul may not have known it, but he was a man of dialectics. For him musical "products" were experiences rather than objects; experiences that made him touch with his own hands, within the concrete world of music, the ever open conflict between subjectivity and objectivity. Truly, he helped musicians in their efforts, yet when those efforts were beginning to show the first wrinkles of "objectivity" and formalism, he would instinctively step back. Often he didn't really know how to step back and hence he could become almost rough. Yet there was a deeper reason for his impatience: the profound, acute awareness that the ultimate meaning of the musical world he wished to build was in reality somewhere else. A "somewhere else" which probably had Jewish roots and which Paul refrained from naming. Another conflict experienced by Paul was the one between the idea of "musical progress" (in terms of *brave new world*) and the temporary loss of meaning sometimes implied in that same "progress." Paul was conscious of the vulnerability of musical experience when it is called to face such conflicts within a social-cultural context that tends to generate irreconcilable antagonisms. He knew, however, that music is fed by conflicts and that it is precisely through striving for synthesis and sublimation of those conflicts that music talks to us also about ourselves. This is why Paul's name shall remain everlastingly tied to the musical creativity of these last thirty-five years.

My first meeting with Paul took place, almost by chance, in 1959. I then came to know him better in the summer of 1960 in Tanglewood, at the time of the first performance by Cathy Berberian of my "Circles," composed for the Fromm Foundation. From then on we remained real friends, even though our meetings were sporadic and mostly occasional. In more recent times we used to talk a lot about wine. His palate was like a computer: he could analyze wines, making an incredibly precise "sampling" of all their parameters.

My last meeting with Paul took place in Chicago on April 12th, 1987; that is, only several days before his hospitalization. On April 14th he had written a letter which was delivered to me by the magnificent Italian mail service only in May. My next letter reached him too late. The tree was no longer there. But its roots are now deep inside of us.

Luciano Berio
February 16, 1988

MEMORIAL TRIBUTES

. . . .

I t is always very encouraging to find personalities like Paul Fromm who are entirely oriented towards the music of our century. He devoted his time and his efforts to this cause, with considerable success, and in spite of all the difficulties one generally encounters in this field.

I remember with gratitude the help he gave us when we put on the 1976 Celebration of Contemporary American Music at the New York Philharmonic and the Juilliard School. He was certainly one of the main forces behind this Festival. Ten years later he helped make possible the first American tour of the Ensemble InterContemporain.

I have always been impressed by Paul's energy and devotion and I wish more people would follow his example.

Pierre Boulez
February 24, 1988

In Memoriam
Paul Fromm

T he loss of Paul Fromm is not only the loss of a wonderful, warm, enthusiastic, intelligent personal friend to so many of us, but it is a loss—a tragic loss—of a unique personal effort that, sadly, appears to have no sequel. In music his was a direct supportive interest in the works of composers themselves. His continual effort to learn, to find out what was worthy and to get behind it by commissioning, by having the music performed, and by having young performers taught to play is indeed remarkable.

Selfless, too, since the reward cannot be measured in the usual financial or even public-relations terms, but only in the works of the composers themselves, for which he will continue to be remembered by an ever-growing group of those who come to know him through his excellently chosen commissions.

Being a private patron of contemporary music now, in our democratic society, is a very unusual role, and one very unlike that of previous times. We do not have the generally agreed-upon cultural patterns once imposed on the general public by a wealthy aristocracy or its bourgeois emulators, those who established music schools, caused instruments to be built and performed upon, and inspired a repertory of musical works to be written to the accompaniment of critical ideologies, as we all know. It is this frozen image of European culture of the past that most American listeners to music expect when they go to concerts or operas.

It took a noble, determined courage for Paul to launch a career as an American patron in these years. For with patrons of previous times, he shared only one quality: that of serious artistic cultivation and concern with the production of good compositions. He did not have the vast wealth or the social position of the Esterhazys, or Ludwig II or the Princesse de Polignac, nor did he command the position of Henry Higginson, the supporter of the Boston Symphony Orchestra in the nineteenth century who insisted that the orchestra play the works of those modernists Brahms and Wagner until the audience liked them. He was not in the heavily supported position of Serge Koussevitzky, who tried to establish an American school of composers like that of the Russian Five, by repeated commissioning and repeated performances of Aaron Copland, Roy Harris, Howard Hanson, William Schuman and others.

Maybe Paul's professional familiarity with the world of wine gave him hope that music, like winemaking, could be transplanted here. For like music, wine has its very elaborate European methods of growing, pruning, pressing, fermenting, aging, and bottling. And like music, its various years, locations, and producers have very different characteristics.

A great judge of wine—he had to be—and of new music, which strongly attracted him, Paul could assess present quality and its ability to improve or deteriorate with time. And best of all, he could generally predict future qualities that would emerge from formative stages. Like one connected with the world of wine, he had great respect in music for careful cultivation, and a conviction that a good product would finally be appreciated. But as with wine, the taste of the consumer had to be cultivated in order to enjoy the result. So he frequently lectured listeners that they should develop their ears by listening to new music and to good new works several times.

He was right, I think, in believing that contemporary music could be appreciated by more than the happy few, as has recently been proved by the sold-out concerts of the Ensemble InterContemporain of Paris or the concerts of our Kronos Quartet, both of which have spent a great deal of time and money and effort on public relations and marketing. This new approach was not considered important during Paul's years, when he continued to believe, as most of us still do, that the good will come to be recognized.

It was a very exciting period to have a man like Paul—one who was not a composer—actively and determinedly espousing our cause. Up to that time, and even now, small groups of composers got together to struggle to organize concerts of their fellows' music. Because of Paul, this activity has now been taken up by some performers, but none of these has the scope of Paul's efforts, which involved starting a new magazine, *Perspectives of New Music*, helping to support the Contemporary Chamber Players here in Chicago, organizing critics' conferences, and giving fellowships to composers and performers at Tanglewood and Aspen to participate in new-music concerts.

All this has been left to ferment, finally to bring forth a large vintage of important American music to a public at last able to appreciate it.

Paul, your efforts, so imaginative and so enthusiastically maintained, have already succeeded in changing the face of our musical culture; we love you for it and are deeply grateful.

Elliott Carter
October 4, 1988*

*These remarks were delivered at a Memorial Service for Paul Fromm held at The University of Chicago on October 4, 1988.

A Remembrance
of Paul Fromm

Let me start at the beginning, which I remember so very well. On March 5, 1960, my son Max was born. Shortly thereafter, while mother and son were still in the hospital, I received a letter from the Fromm Foundation, which is to say, from Paul Fromm, offering me my first Fromm commission. Was this more than a coincidence? I don't know. The result of that commission was my *Dimensions* for soprano and twenty-three instruments, written in 1960. The piece was subsequently performed in New York under my baton on an entire program of Fromm commissions at the New School, which was then on 10th Street. My first physical encounter with Paul Fromm took place on that occasion. From 1960 to 64, although living in Chicago, Paul always kept in touch with whatever I was doing as a composer and conductor.

In 1964, I came to The University of Chicago. I remember that at the time of my interview here, I felt that I couldn't impose upon Paul Fromm, that I couldn't call Paul Fromm. He was a patron and one couldn't bother a patron. How silly I was became apparent when Paul called me. Paul picked me up at Lenny Meyer's where I was staying. Within a few minutes, after the usual greetings, Paul began to talk about the job being offered at the University of Chicago. He spontaneously gave me advice about the job, advice that proved invaluable. Subsequently, I came to the University of Chicago as a composer, joining the staff with an assistant professorship. There, in 1964, I founded the Contemporary Chamber Players of the University of Chicago.

While Paul had nothing whatsoever to do with any of this, he later proved a good friend to The Contemporary Players. For one thing, he came to all our concerts. Two years passed, and, in 1966, Paul said, "Ralph, I want to speak to you." We were invited to dinner. This was a very important dinner for me, because Paul said to me, "From now on, you will conduct a Fromm concert in Chicago." It was very obvious that he had waited to see how good we were and what kind of programs we would put on before deciding to invite us to do these annual concerts. Over the years now—for twenty-two of the twenty-four years that I've been here—we have continued to put on Fromm concerts.

Each year Paul and I would meet to discuss the program until arriving at a mutual understanding as to the format of the program. Many times I would go home to figure out a ball-park figure for the amount that the concert would cost the Foundation, only to discover that a program was going to go way over budget. I would call Paul to tell him that we were going to have to change the program. "*Ach*, really? Why?" he would ask, and I would respond that the ball-park figure for the budget was too high. He would laugh and say, "We make no changes." Paul often remarked that I was more worried about his money than he was.

I once said to Paul that we were involved in an expensive hobby. It made no difference to him. This was one of his passions; this was his mission in life: to give composers, and especially young composers, a chance to show what they can do. This was done primarily through commissions, and, beyond commissions, through ensuring that commissioned works were performed under the best possible conditions. Everyone wanted a Fromm commission. It was and is a very prestigious commission. If you received a Fromm commission, you waved the flag, because everyone knew that this was a very important step in your life as a composer.

I refrained from becoming involved in Foundation activities other than those concerning my Chicago concerts. It was sufficient for me to phone Paul and ask him to commission someone. Whether it was a young composer just emerging or an established figure, Paul never disagreed. Sometimes I would suggest that some famous composer had never received a Fromm commission and that this composer, whether or not we liked his or her music, was worthy of the recognition of a Fromm commission. Inevitably, Paul would commission a work.

I recall a commissioned work that made me very angry. The work was by George Rochberg, and, since we do have certain expectations, I had expected a certain kind of work such as he had been writing for many years. Rochberg was on the verge of his period of quotations and this particular work contained some thirty pages of quotations from a Mozart E flat Divertimento. I was mad as hell, saying that if I wanted to conduct Mozart, I could conduct Mozart without doing it via George Rochberg. Paul let me blow my stack. He sat listening as I ranted and raved before saying, "Ralph, we commissioned a work from a composer, and he has a perfect right to experiment; he has a right to change. Ralph, you will do the work and you will do it beautifully." Of course, Paul was right.

Over the years, Paul and I became very close friends. Many times my phone would ring and I would hear Paul's inimitable accent: "*Ach*, Ralph! When I want the truth I come to you." And I always told Paul, "You know, Paul, the truth—this is *my* truth. I can only tell you what I think or what I believe."

Since this is a remembrance by Ralph Shapey, I have to tell you of my own personal debt to Paul. I believe that I may be one of the few composers to have received more than one commission. As a matter of fact, the total comes to three commissions. I didn't ask for them. I didn't want them, but Paul insisted that I receive them. As I have so often stated, he believed in me when nobody else believed in me. Paul stood behind me when no one else wanted me. He insisted on sending my various scores to the prize committees. This happened even shortly before he died. I told Paul that it wasn't worth the aggravation, but he insisted, saying, "Ralph, some day we are going to break through that gang." Paul, you're not here anymore to break through that gang, but I thank you deeply from my heart for being such a dear friend and for standing behind me when no one else did. Furthermore, I know that there are numerous other composers who feel as I do. They will all speak for Paul Fromm.

Paul was always there: the patron, but even more than the patron, the friend. I have some idea of just how many composers turned to Paul for advice, who sought him out in their time of need. Proverbially, his generosity knew no bounds, but his support went well beyond the financial. I am firmly convinced that many of the hopeful signs on the musical horizon are due to his influence: the establishment of residencies for composers with major symphony orchestras, the proliferation of prizes and competitions, the increased number of commissions available from sources other than the Fromm Foundation. This is the man who fought for the composer, who believed that the composer must occupy a privileged position within our society. Paul indefatigably lectured to symphony orchestras, to boards of symphony orchestras, and to audiences with one constant theme: the living composer should be at the very center of a vital musical culture. Paul single-handedly changed the world of composition in America.

When I composed my Fromm Variations for Piano and dedicated them to Paul, I know that he was touched, because he said to me, "Now I will be an asterisk in the history books." I laughed, but this shows how modest Paul could be. At concerts, when asked to take a bow, Paul always refused. As he so often said, "The composer takes the bow, not the patron." We did manage to get him on his feet on more than one occasion, though, because this was a man who loved us and who proved his love to us and to the world. Wherever you may be, Paul, we will never forget you. Believe me, you are going to be one hell of an asterisk in the history books.

Ralph Shapey
February 24, 1988

SELECTED
PAPERS of
PAUL FROMM

New Music:
Is There Really a Crisis?

These remarks were first delivered in August of 1972 at Tanglewood as part of the celebration of the Fromm Foundation's twentieth anniversary. They were subsequently printed in the Musical America *section of* High Fidelity/Musical America *(v. 22, no. 12, pp. 11 & 28) in December 1982.*

T he musical community has acknowledged the twentieth anniversary of the Fromm Foundation so genuinely and so generously that I now feel a little like Mae West when she said: "Too much of a good thing is wonderful." I was waiting for someone to tell us where we failed, and as nobody did, I will now take on this task myself.

I am concerned about our failure, not in activity, but in aim. By this I mean that we have carried on our work with rather naive hopes as to its eventual effect on the contemporary art scene.

Six years ago when I addressed this audience—it was the occasion of the tenth anniversary of the association between the Fromm Foundation and the Berkshire Music Center—I spoke of the co-existence of separate audiences for contemporary music and the music of the past as a state of affairs implying some kind of cold war and involving a second-class existence for contemporary music. I hoped that it was only temporary; indeed, as I had characterized it, coexistence could only be temporary, and any kind of integration between the two musics and their audiences seemed better than the fragmentation that mere coexistence would engender.

I am embarrassed now at my rather glib use of the words "coexistence" and "integration" at that time. Coexistence with its political overtones had an altogether negative connotation and integration could not then have been viewed other than positively. By now we have begun to recognize that integration means more than shoving two things together, and we may even have learned that a pluralistic society is large enough to contain coexisting variety.

We all have experienced the typical orchestral concert in which an insignificant new work is insinuated into a program containing the Brahms Second Piano Concerto and the Beethoven Seventh Symphony. The Brahms and Beethoven lovers are irritated beyond endurance by the new work. The listeners who have come for the new piece are annoyed by the presentation of a weak example of contemporary literature and are bored by being over-exposed to the music of Brahms and Beethoven. Frequently, the limitations of the rehearsal schedule demand that the new work take up most of the rehearsal time and masterworks of the past are given under-rehearsed, indifferent performances. This irritates the traditionalists still further, and they blame contemporary music for an uneventful evening. Moreover, an audience of Brahms and Beethoven lovers that hears a contemporary work of much lesser musical stature than the works with which it has been programmed, can become so completely prejudiced against the whole idea of new music that it would be better for the reputation of contemporary music if the piece had not been played. This sort of mere busing of indiscriminately chosen new music to the halls of Brahms and Beethoven is surely not integration. I must remind you that in a reverse situation, Beethoven's greatness would be momentarily eclipsed if his feeble *Battle* Symphony would appear on the same program with Carter's Variations for Orchestra and Stravinsky's *Rite of Spring*. "The great mistake," as Pierre Boulez noted, "is trying to devise menus to please everybody. That ends with all stomachs upset."

We have created the problem in part by pitting the audience for new music against the audience for music of the past. This is a false dichotomy. Music lovers don't really divide themselves chronologically or even that simply. They divide in two separate but mutually inclusive ways: adventurous listeners, and listeners who are seeking merely an emotional experience, as against listeners who are seeking both an emotional and intellectual experience. Thus, we have both conservative and adventurous music enthusiasts and both conservative and adventurous—shall we say—musical intelligentsia.

New music obviously attracts both kinds of adventurous listeners; but new music can mean not only contemporary music but also music that is new to that listener. That is, music with which he has not been surfeited—the neglected symphonies of Mozart and Haydn, most of the music of Johann Sebastian Bach, Renaissance polyphony, medieval music played on old instruments, oriental music. All of this is in that sense new music. The audience for contemporary music is frequently found at concerts of old non-nineteenth-century works or performances including the nineteenth-century rarities. I could name quite a number of musicians, among them Boulez, Maderna, Ozawa, Schuller, and Michael Tilson Thomas, who have found the ideal concert format for this audience. They created coherence in programming by the performance of works of different styles and periods, which have the power to illuminate each other. That is real integration.

I have made a point of considering the conservative but intelligent music lover as someone quite distinct from the conservative music enthusiast because there is a prevailing attitude among the contemporary music elite that anyone who is conservative can't be intelligent. This is, of course, patently untrue. The intelligent conservative must be taken seriously. In the musical context, he holds out against what he thinks might be mere faddism and guards himself against a certain kind of esthetic promiscuity. This is honorable. His resistance grows in part out of bewilderment and, I think, this is the bewilderment that most of us have shared to some extent. Viewing the history of Western music, he has observed that it is a history of dominant styles. So he asks himself which of the current proliferation of twentieth-century styles will prove to be triumphant?

For the conservative music lover and for the conservative part in all of us, there may be some comfort in the idea that if we are living in a pluralistic society, as historians, social scientists, and philosophers increasingly believe that we are, then perhaps none of these styles will be finally dominant. They will, instead, all coexist, for they will not be threatened by each other—the new will not displace but be added on. The styles of late romanticism, primitivism, neoclassicism, aleatoric, and totally or partially organized music have appeared to succeed one another in the twentieth century, but that is an illusion. They have all continued in one form or another. None has really disappeared or been replaced. If, as it is now quite widely recognized, the present pluralism of coexisting styles is not a transitional state but a permanent condition, then the audience will have time to absorb styles and develop criteria for evaluating them. If that is so, then we may not be in a state of crisis.

The Arts
in the Seventies

This address was originally presented as part of the series "Music in American Life" at the Peabody Institute in Baltimore on April 19, 1978. A version of this paper was published later that year in the October issue of The New Art Examiner *(v. 6, no. 11) as "Cultural Retreat of the 70's." The original paper is printed here.*

B efore the 1976 presidential election campaigners of both political persuasions went about asking, "When are the Seventies going to begin?" It was not entirely a rhetorical question. The decade, which was then already more than half over, still had not established any positive identity as a decade. Vietnam and then Watergate and then the economic recession had diverted our attention from the optimism of the early and middle Sixties—the optimism of the New Frontier and of the Great Society. The high hopes for achieving social justice for all and progress in education and in the arts had been exhausted. In place of social concern, we are preoccupied with our own concerns. The need to be involved had been transformed into the desire to withdraw into ourselves.

The Sixties had been more than bewildering in its parade of various and often conflicting attitudes, styles, fashions, trends. And nowhere was the range of variety, the polarity, greater than in the arts. Yet the Seventies have been far more perplexing than the Sixties. The one thing that seems clear is that what is going on now can only be understood in reference to the events of the Sixties. In his new collection of essays, Gore Vidal reports a conversation that he had with Tennessee Williams a year or two ago. When Williams confessed to Vidal, "I slept through the Sixties," Vidal responded facetiously, "You didn't miss a thing." Then he added in a more sober afterthought, "But if you missed the Sixties, God knows what you are going to do with the Seventies."

Even for those of us who remained more or less awake during the Sixties, the Seventies are confusing! Insofar as we considered the Sixties wonderfully lively, energetic, creative, involving, the Seventies have simply been dull, not so much a change from the Sixties as empty, tried repetition of Sixties-style events. As one writer put it, "The big wave of the Sixties broke in the earliest Seventies. [For awhile, we] paddled about in its froth. That same water is now tranquil and flat."

Insofar as we found the events of the Sixties turbulent, the Seventies are an aftermath. As at the end of a Shakespearean tragedy, the bodies are being taken up, things are being righted, some kind of order is being restored.

What is perplexing is that these impressions are not just different subjective interpretations of the same phenomena. The phenomena themselves contain the contradiction. In the arts, at any rate, there is, on the one hand, a dull continuity from the Sixties, a sense that we are being urged to eat Sixties leftovers. This is because many of the innovations of the Sixties have found their way into mass entertainment and continue as empty forms. On the other hand, a conservative reaction against the Sixties has also set in. The theater is once again the home of the well-made play. And in architecture, painting, sculpture, and music, too, the search for order is leading artists into the past.

Let's look first at the way in which the Seventies are continuing the arts of the Sixties. Our arts today are, if I may paraphrase Hamlet, weary, stale, flat but *not unprofitable*. What has happened is that we have finally discovered the business potential in the arts. This shouldn't be surprising. It has long been pointed out that we are a nation of hustlers, rather than makers. The amazing thing is that it took so long.

Of course, the commercial exploitation of the arts was widely happening in the Sixties. But at that time we felt that we were standing on the threshold of something important. There was tremendous activity—not only audience expansion and the building of cultural centers of all kinds, but also a proliferation of new forms and styles in the arts themselves. It looked as if we were living not only in a period of vast consumption of the arts but in a creative era as well. We have probably never been so aware of the range and variety of our society and its tastes in the arts as we were in the Sixties.

Up until then we had been straining to perceive which forms and styles were going to be dominant in our century. Gradually, it occurred to us that the flow of artistic creation would no longer have to direct itself into a mainstream in order to keep from drying out. The climate seemed agreeable enough that there could be many separate channels. We began to realize that we lived in a pluralistic society and that this pluralism included the arts, that there would be room for many different styles to exist harmoniously—or not so harmoniously—alongside each other. Perhaps the most extraordinary development was what was suddenly happening to motion pictures—a trend that turned out to be only temporary. Movies had been the mass entertainment of all mass entertainments. But in the Sixties when television had established itself as *the* mass entertainment, movie makers started diversifying, making different kinds of films for different audiences. As a result, American movies in the Sixties were more exciting artistically than they had been before the advent of the television age. There certainly were some warning signs in the Sixties. We were aware even then that the phrase "cultural explosion" had a destructive sound. Some of us even figured out that when managers of arts organizations used the phrase "audience development," they weren't talking about helping audiences go through a process of growth, differentiation and evolution vis-à-vis the arts. They were really talking about corralling ticket buyers. We had long known that the most difficult distinction for people in this country to make is that "something for everyone" is not the same as "everything for everyone." We also realized that there was a great deal of crossover between serious art and commercial entertainment. Abetted by the media, many innovations in the arts also became popular entertainments. Artists were becoming celebrities, a distinction previously reserved for show business personalities. Even so, for the first time the no-man's land between serious art and popular entertainment seemed permanently habitable. And there was enough money around that even the unpopular innovations could find support, could float along on the general tide of excitement about the arts.

Meanwhile, many arts operations had transformed themselves into businesses, had put themselves into the hands of commercial entrepreneurs. We had encouraged this, let's not forget. Remember when we used to complain that one of the problems of orchestras and museums and theaters and opera and dance companies was that they were not businesslike enough, that they lacked managerial finesse? We even had foundation-supported programs for training arts managers. And so while we were exulting in the pluralistic arts of the Sixties, the businessmen and women of the arts began learning their trade. They became dealers in commodities for pre-sold buyers—for subscription audiences. They learned to evaluate artistic activity like any other product, for its impact upon the consumer rather than for any intrinsic merit. They discovered that it was possible to confer artistic prestige upon a person or a work or an event simply through promotion. Danny Newman, who is Director of Public Relations for Lyric Opera of Chicago and a consultant to many arts institutions in this country and in Canada, has probably worked harder and with greater success than any other single person to promote the concept of the pre-sold subscription audience. He now has a book out, called *Subscribe Now!* It is significant that the title of this book is a command that ends with an exclamation point. In the book Newman identifies his method as Dynamic Sales Promotion and then uses the initials DSP to refer to it thereafter. I think it is symptomatic that arts managers are by now proud of the sales techniques that they have put to use. They no longer hide behind euphemisms like "audience development." They don't have to because when in the early Seventies, times got bad, the only arts that continued to expand were the ones that had become—to a greater or lesser degree—business. Regardless of the recession, the art market was continuing to inflate. Joseph Epstein pointed to the imcompatible relationship between business and the arts when he wrote in *The American Scholar:*

> Business is about profit; culture is about standards and taste. Although one likes to think of the two coalescing in purpose, more often they are at cross purposes. In any standoff competition between the two, culture goes down nearly every time.

It's interesting how the peculiar combination of *inflation* and *recession* that is the economic condition of our society as a whole also accounts for what is happening in the arts, although here we must use these terms at least partly as metaphors.

We have *inflation* in the sense that there is a continuing increase in arts consumption. The National Endowment for the Arts and Humanities has announced that between 1965 and 1975, professional orchestras doubled, resident professional theaters quadrupled, arts councils quintupled, and resident professional dance companies increased sevenfold. Some of this expansion occurred in the Sixties, but much of it has come in the Seventies.

As a result, more people than ever before are aware of the arts, ironically enough, more people in this relatively duller period than in the more brilliant Sixties. A Harris Poll taken less than two years ago reports that eighty-nine percent of Americans agree that the arts are important to the quality of life.

Unfortunately, just as people are becoming more aware of the arts as entertainment, just as the arts business is *inflating,* we are experiencing a *recession* in the arts as arts. Few if any new forms are being created and many of the experiments of the Sixties—the innovations of the Living Theater, electronic music, aleatoric music, action painting, multi-media works—to name a few—have gone stale or vanished, or where remnants of them persist, in popular works, they have become neutralized so that audiences no longer feel their charge.

Increasingly, our arts are becoming neutralized, one might even say, homogenized. American business taught us a long time ago that mass production demands standardization. So now in the arts that are most successful, there is a kind of erosion going on, a smoothing out of differences, a subtle neglect of detail, a limiting of choices. At none of the hamburger chains can you expect to have your ground beef served to you on Baltic rye with Dijon mustard instead of on a mushy white bun. And our arts organizations seem more and more to be in the fast food business. Instead of many arts organizations that represent many points of view, we have producers who have no point of view. This is standardization, not in the sense of maintaining high standards, but of keeping products uniform, of trying to please some hypothetical common denominator.

The field of dance offers the most interesting example of this standardization process. Dance, which for three decades was ignored by the American public, has become the most successful, the most popular, of the arts of the Seventies. During the time it was ignored, dance had been the stronghold of individual styles. Dancers created dances as exclusive vehicles for themselves or their own companies. One would never think, for example, of Martha Graham creating a work for herself that could also be performed by the Joffrey Ballet. In the early days, dancers went around from studio to studio to find a technique that fit them. Now, most of the techniques are borrowed, hand-me-down, a little of this and a little of that. The idea now is to produce a breed of dancer who is adaptable, who can move from ballet to modern dance and back again, rather than a more focused, but admittedly limited dancer. And choreographers with companies of their own now also make new dances for other companies. All this sharing has led to a breakdown of individual styles. As a result, dance is creating a popular version of itself—an all-purpose, technically stunning, but stylistically bland kind of dancing that appeals to the new audience for dance, an audience that is impressed by athletic feats, by flashiness, and even by distortion, an audience that has very little anchorage in the past.

Perhaps this is also what has been going on in performances by our symphony orchestras for quite some time. Our orchestras developed a broader audience before dance companies did. If rock has been the popular music for the very young, perhaps nineteenth-century symphonies have functioned as the pop music of their elders. An important distinction needs to be made here. It is not the musical works themselves that are pop, but the approach that is taken to their performance. In our orchestra concerts, as in pop dance performances, a technically brilliant performance is valued far more than a stylistically penetrating one. In such showy performances Haydn begins to sound like Beethoven. These works no longer relate to the periods in which they were created. We have also numbed concert audiences by constant repetition of an increasingly smaller number of works. These works have now become the "top forty" of the traditional musical establishment.

This doesn't mean that we never hear stylistically acute performances of music, just as it doesn't mean that good books, good works of art, theater, music, and dance are no longer being produced. But, unfortunately, the good works tend to get lost amid the mediocre. And in all the clutter, it becomes more and more difficult to tell the good from the bad. Simply because the sheer quantity of art being produced is bewildering, arts *inflation* is working against the arts, contributing toward our sense of *receding* quality.

The unhappy mating of *inflation* and *recession* in the arts can also be seen in what's happening to the arts in education. Our national eagerness for commercial expansion of the arts is not matched by an interest in arts education. The same Harris Poll that found eighty-nine percent of us agreeing that arts are important to the quality of life also found that only thirty-nine percent think it's important that children learn about some of the great contributors to art and literature.

In the Sixties as the commercial expansion of the arts began, as artists' names became household words, as the arts themselves divided and multiplied and grew diverse enough to serve all tastes (and aid all causes), there seemed to be every promise that arts education would take root. In spite of this, the arts somehow never managed to achieve any status in our schools beyond that of frills. Consequently, when the economic pinch and the call for educational accountability hit schools at the same time, the arts went out the door. It didn't help that the most trivial—least basic—manifestations of art in the Sixties had received the biggest play in the media. And so when it came time for the "back to the basics" movement, the arts were not seen as basic.

The results are devastating. In New York City, for example, all specialists in music and art have been eliminated from the city's 600 elementary schools. In New York's high schools two-thirds of the art teachers and one-third of the music teachers are gone. I'm not quite sure why music should fare better than art in New York high shcools. Perhaps administrators feel that they do need band directors to lead the half-time activities at football and basketball games. I mention New York City only as an example. What has happened there is no different from what has happened in schools all over the country. Who would want to question that the arts do belong among the basics? Instead of reducing the number of art and music teachers, we should be expanding the concept of literacy to include the language of gesture, image, sound, and movement. We should even be adding dance appreciation to the curriculum.

Still another way of viewing the peculiar combination of *inflation* and *recession,* or *shrinkage,* in the arts is to consider the place of the artist in society. We have made artists into stars, into celebrities. We've *inflated* their stock in the sense of making them richer, more popular, more famous than they've ever been. Does this mean that people today value the artist more than ever before? I don't think so. One of the most persistent residual attitudes from the revolutionary Sixties is that of anti-elitism. Ironically enough, the very arts that were being used to proclaim egalitarian slogans in the Sixties have now fallen victim to these slogans. The egalitarianism of the Sixties has lost its social forcefulness. But anti-elitism remains and has turned back on art itself. People quietly—sometimes not so quietly—believe that you shouldn't trust the artist. Just a few months ago Senator Claiborne Pell was quoted in the *New York Times* as saying that the National Endowment has been wasting its money supporting intellectuals in projects that do not benefit most of the people.

The Arts Establishment believes that artists can't be trusted because as creators, as innovators, they are unpredictable. They can't be easily managed or led, can't be counted on to bring forth what everyone will like. The very existence of artists refutes the belief that all persons can do all things. In that sense, artists are undemocratic.

By transforming artists into stars, however, we can make them manipulable. We, the audience, can get them into our power. Anyone who can be manipulated can be trusted. And so we trust stars in a way that we don't trust artists. At the same time we also feel contempt for stars and celebrities. I believe it was Eric Larrabee who first defined the term *celebrity* by saying it consists in being famous for being famous. The implication is that once you're a celebrity, you don't have to work so hard at being an artist any more. After all, a celebrity is someone who is required to spend most of his time making personal appearances. Tom Wolfe has carried the grain of truth in this definition to its logical extremes by concluding that the intellectual center of the United States is now O'Hare Airport. On any day, Monday through Friday, September through June, explains Wolfe, from one-tenth to one-third of the artists and intellectuals of the United States are sitting in the black vinyl and stainless steel Mies van der Rohe chairs at O'Hare, waiting for connecting flights. They're heading out into the land to make public appearances. And in the peak months, October and April, the number goes up to one-half!

To illustrate his contention, Tom Wolfe shares the following experience:

> At a literary conference at Notre Dame, I ran into a poet who is noted for his verse celebrating the ecology. [In an earlier time, he would be called a nature poet.] He lives in a dramatic house nailed together completely from uncut pieces of hickory driftwood, perched on a bluff overlooking the crashing ocean, a spot so remote that you can drive no closer than five miles to it by conventional automobile and barely within a mile and a half by Jeep. The last 7,500 feet it's hand over hand up rocks, vines, and lengths of hemp. I remarked that this must be the ideal setting in which to write about the ecological wonders.
>
> "I wouldn't know," he said. "I do all my writing at O'Hare."

Of course, the insidious result of getting artists into our power by making celebrities out of them is that we stunt their artistic development. We typecast them in the media, and then condemn them if they don't follow what is expected of the type. They become mere replaceable commodities.

In a way it is ironic that it is arts consumerism that threatens to control and destroy the artist. Artists used to be wary of government arts subsidies. They were afraid of direct government control of artistic content. This has not occurred. Instead, arts funding has quietly linked itself into the industry of arts consumerism. Subsidies have become increasingly dependent on the size of an arts organization's budget, the number of people it employs and the size of the audience it serves.

Initially, the government granting agencies seemed to be foresighted in feeding the flow of new ideas by giving small amounts of money to young experimental artists.

But now that money is tight and we are plagued with unemployment, arts subsidies have become the means, not so much of developing the arts themselves, as of creating arts-related jobs and stimulating consumer spending. One of President Carter's arts consultants, Louise Wiener, announced early last year that "The prime concern of the government has got to be the economy and jobs and you have to look at the whole place of the arts in our economic life in order to understand their significance. The government should be sensitive to how it can help the commercial area as well as the nonprofit."

Unfortunately, subsidy based on number—on quantitative appraisals—does not stimulate new artists; it encourages opportunists.

It is tempting to consider the Seventies retreat into the past as one more example of the *inflation-recession* syndrome in the arts. And the popular side of this retreat—the nostalgia boom—is just that. In a time when the arts have grown almost frantically commercial, when art is defined as anything that will sell, when the arts that sell best are the ones that receive government subsidization, when the emphasis is on playing safe, when audiences want easy, instantly comprehensible art that demands little from them, then the old, familiar entertainments seem like good bets—turn of the century *verismo* opera, landscape painting, realistic problem plays and romantic ballet.

Of course, to us who are primarily interested in music, nostalgia and the retreat to the art of the past on the part of the audience is anything but a new syndrome. I found it amusing in a sad sort of way a few Sundays ago to glance into the Arts Section of the *Chicago Tribune* and discover a theater reviewer, Linda Winer, asking, "Why do we have to use the word *revive* whenever someone mounts a new production of *My Fair Lady* or *Oklahoma*? After all," she argued, "when symphony orchestras perform Beethoven's *Ninth Symphony*, they don't say they're reviving it; they just announce that they're planning to play it." She's perfectly right. We don't talk about reviving Beethoven. But then you can't very well revive something that you've never laid aside. In a sense, the field of music has now, suddenly, distinguished itself in a way none of us had ever hoped it would. For years, for the entire century, music has lagged behind the other arts—at least behind painting and sculpture and architecture—in terms of audience acceptance of its most advanced manifestations. In the Fifties that astute social observer, Marya Mannes, described the typical smart New York home as follows: "A Jackson Pollock over the mantel, a Henry Moore sculpture in the corner, a book of contemporary poetry on the coffee table and Vivaldi on the phonograph." Now, finally, music audiences are in the lead, even if they are merely leading a retreat. Seriously though, the current backlash in the arts, that wave of cultural nostalgia, is related to a seriously retrospective mood on the part of our artists. It is difficult to know whether this retreat is the cause or the effect of our current lack of artistic adventurousness and forward striving.

What does seem clear is that there are two kinds of reactions. One is a rebellion against *severity* in the arts. This reaction is most evident in the field of architecture although it has parallels in painting and music. Architects raised on Mies van der Rohe's famous dictum, "Less is More," are hungrily grasping for a little more. Among the younger generation of architects there is a feeling that modern architecture was an abstract art that failed to meet practical human needs. One might say the same about some of the most arid examples of music. But *severity* is a more immediate problem in architecture because people must live and work in buildings. Music is easier to ignore. As several recent exhibits of architectural drawings show, architects are no longer drawing plain grids plotted with rigid correct lines. Instead the new drawings have vibrant colors, free-flowing lines, and even whimsical and poetic commentary. There is a feeling of luxuriating in the art of the past. As *New York Times* architecture critic Ada Louise Huxtable has characterized it, the movement is "a romantic revivalism that accommodates both the most superficial nostalgic kitsch and the most informed historicism."

The other kind of conservative reaction stems from a realization that much of what passed for avant garde in the Sixties, and even later, has proved to be extremely *trivial*. The appetite for music played on barbecue trays and glasses of water and brake drums, for performers smacking each other in the face, paint indiscriminately hurled at the canvas, for shocks and assaults on the audience, has diminished. At first these happenings seemed a refreshing change from a previous emphasis on structure. But eventually people got tired of these goings-on—artists as well as members of their audiences. They were not really interesting either visually or as sound. And they were briefly "surprising" only in that we never expected such antics in a concert hall or museum.

The curious thing is that the ultra-severe art now seems to lack substance just as surely as does obviously trivial art. The theories behind some of the most determinedly intellectual works of art and music were so fascinating to the mind that, for a while, we ignored the fact that often the works themselves were barren. Consequently, part of the conservative movement in the arts has as its purpose "to put the paint back into the painting," or to put sound back into music.

The similarity of these reactions—both against extreme developments that have diminished artistic substance—suggests that the retreat into the past may only be an attempt on the part of our culture to regain its balance. It is a historical fact that the revival of historical styles has seldom led to major artistic statements. It may be that this period of retreat coming after a time of experimentation is a prelude to a time of sorting out. Artists may be bracing themselves for the real artistic struggle of separating the consequential from the inconsequential. It may be that the retreat into the past is not really an escape at all. Instead, it may be a recovery from what was in the Sixties an attempt to escape into the future, to ignore tradition. Lukas Foss once pointed out that if we try to plunge headlong into the future without having sunk our roots deeply into the past, it is just as surely a form of escape as getting stuck in the past. It is, he said, what Pierre Boulez once aptly called *"la fuite en avant,"* an escape forward. Likewise, Elliott Carter has written, "Awareness of tradition provides not only a way of carrying on but also a way of turning away." We may need this time to find our roots, to learn where we've been so that we can go forward.

Rather than focus on contemporary music as a separate entity and activity, I have attempted to give you an overview of the arts in the Seventies, an account that is admittedly highly personal and perhaps even biased. I *am* deeply pessimistic about the current state of the arts, as my observations and reflections show only too well. But that does not mean that I am entirely without hope for the future. Contradictory as it sounds, the arts may finally be saved by the very fact that in a technological society they are reduced to a peripheral role. Indeed, it appears that the arts with the highest prospects for creative development are the ones that have the least likelihood of being grabbed up by promoters and transformed into mass entertainment. As we approach the Eighties, we can only hope that all the arts will be freed from institutional domination and be returned to the artists themselves. That might be the beginning of a new golden age when the makers, doers, and consumers of the arts will again become active participants in the artistic process. Marcel Duchamp once said: "The artist is only one aspect of the creative process. The spectator—by his active response—completes the cycle."

Twentieth-Century Music:
Trouble Along the Road
to the Twenty-First Century

This lecture was given at the Eastman School of Music, University of Rochester, Rochester, New York, on April 5, 1979.

As long as I have been given several roles to choose from, I think I would just as soon not appear before you today as a representative of a foundation or a patron of music. Everyone knows that any ideas expressed by a patron are worthless unless they are accompanied by the cash necessary to make them persuasive. Remember, when Molière's *Le Bourgeois Gentilhomme* became an active patron of the arts, it was said of him, and this is my own free translation:

His money makes up for the poor judgments of his mind.

His critical faculties can all be found in his wallet.

You see, a patron is rather like an heiress who can never be sure that her suitors love her for herself. Or, and this is far more insidious, like an heiress who assumes that because she has so many suitors, she necessarily possesses intrinsic merit.

So let me speak to you today, not as the voice of the Fromm Music Foundation, not as a patron of music, but just as a member of the audience for twentieth-century music, and, necessarily, a concerned member.

In the Middle Ages, treatises on music often contained elaborate allegories in which music and the other liberal arts were personified. I would like to use an allegory, but a much simpler one, to talk about twentieth-century music.

Imagine twentieth-century music as a figure seated in a carriage. You can furnish out the details of this figure for yourselves. You may see twentieth-century music as a radiant goddess, or as a stern taskmaster, or even as an impudent or difficult child, whatever delights your fancy. Twentieth-century music is taking a dangerous journey—it's a journey to the twenty-first century—in a carriage pulled by three pairs of steeds. These three pairs of steeds are—in the order of their proximity to music's carriage—composers, performers, and patrons. There is much arguing among the steeds, who, because this is an allegory, can talk and think and do anything we want them to do. They are arguing over which of them is responsible for the fact that twentieth-century music is not getting a smooth ride. Out front, the patrons keep stopping and looking back at the performers who keep stopping and looking back at the composers who keep stopping and looking back at the carriage. Sometimes, it seems to the composers that the carriage is empty, that there is no driver. Other times, the composers so chafe under music's whip that they feel they cannot tolerate the slow pace of the other steeds; they must break loose and bolt, pulling the carriage by themselves. It is clear to anyone observing from a distance that if all three pairs of steeds would pull their own weight, without worrying about what the others are doing, twentieth-century music would have a much less precipitous journey. There would still be the danger of being forced to travel through regions populated by ignorant, backward, and hostile tribes, as well as frequent attacks by, shall we call them professional badmen. But these external dangers could be much more easily withstood if music were not also in constant danger of falling out of the carriage.

My entire message to you today is summed up in this little allegory, but allow me to follow another medieval practice and provide a gloss on our text. Let me try to explain its implications in some detail, to indicate how each pair of steeds—patrons, performers, and composers, has faltered and suggest how each might better contribute toward twentieth-century music's well-being along the way to the twenty-first century.

Let's talk first about patrons. We have just experienced a period of nearly two decades during which arts patronage went big time. Private foundations, public agencies, and, eventually, even some corporations finally turned their attention to music and the other performing arts. For the first time in American history, music became both an object of organized philanthropy and a responsibility of the social welfare state. We have had what amounts to a patronage boom.

There are a number of ways to evaluate this development. Viewed in purely financial terms at the most general level, organized arts patronage appears to be continuing and even increasing.

However, the situation is not so bright as this sounds, even from a financial standpoint. Our two major foundations have drastically reduced their arts programs. The Ford Foundation has lowered its annual spending in the arts from a high point of $20 million to $4 million (a reduction of eighty percent). And the recent appointment of Franklin Thomas as the new President of the Ford Foundation suggests that the Foundation will be placing more emphasis on urban problems and even less on the arts. The Rockefeller Foundation, another former mainstay of arts support, gave nearly $35 million in 1972, but only $2 million in 1976, with $1.4 million of that $2 million going to Rockefeller's own American Recording Society project.

One reason for this decline is simply that these foundations now have much less money to spend than they had in the sixties. Still, the decline in arts support is disproportionate to this overall decline. I fear that the decline in the arts program has come about at least partly because the people at Ford and Rockefeller feel that any grants they can now make are trivial alongside the huge allocations of the National Endowment for the Arts and of the state arts councils. This is, of course, understandable. If a large part of your influence has been due to the sheer quantity of your giving, suddenly having much less money to work with would tend to make you feel powerless. Actually, without seeming to be too immodest, I'd like to tell Ford and Rockefeller that the Fromm Foundation has been making "trivial" grants for twenty-five years, and I believe we have had—and are still having—an impact on the contemporary music scene. We've tried to do what we could with a relatively small amount of money which, in every phase of our program, we have put at the service of personal commitment. I would hope that our two major foundations will not fall victim to the notion that government agencies and corporations can take over what the foundations started.

Regardless of the size of the National Endowment's budget, support of the arts is one area in which government can never play more than a secondary role. If our arts are to be encouraged as they should be, private foundations will have to play not only a larger, but a more imaginative and innovative role. Both government and business have too limited a view of what the arts are about. They consider the arts a phenomenon to be exploited for economic or social, and hence, political goals.

To stimulate consumer spending in the arts and create or continue arts-related jobs, the National Endowment primarily assists arts organizations that have large budgets and can report large numbers of ticket buyers. To put it differently, popular success is a prerequisite for aid. This sort of arts patronage reminds me of Samuel Johnson's definition of a patron. Dr. Johnson once asked Lord Chesterfield, "Is not a patron, my Lord, one who looks with unconcern on a man struggling for life in the water, and, when he has reached ground, encumbers him with help?"

Of the twelve divisions funded by the National Endowment, only six could even properly be called arts. The others include marginal endeavors with populist appeal like folk arts, handicrafts, inner city community activity, and ethnic programs.

Let's turn to state government. The New York State Council on the Arts, whose budget is larger than the budgets of all other state councils combined, is required to distribute its money on a per capita basis in each county throughout the state. As a result, the council is made to give its money not in proportion to where art flourishes, but to where it doesn't flourish or where it does not even exist.

As for corporate support for the arts, it tends to be little more than a dignified form of institutional advertising. Most corporate money is being used to sponsor televised music, theater, and dance programs, generally chosen for their mass appeal. And, as Lincoln Kirstein characterized sponsored arts programs on television, "Big advertisers will not allow you to be left with an artistic vision superior to that of Mobil or Exxon."

On the local level, businesses give money to glamorous artistic enterprises in the belief that the arts should be cultivated to help tourism or because having cultural resources in a city is somehow "good for business." Businesses are also learning that they can find ways to bask in the reflected glow of an eminent cultural institution.

I think it is clear why the arts continue to need independent foundation funding even if at a reduced level. The foundations have the capacity—because they are independent—to regard the arts as arts, not as political and social pawns. And as imaginative programs in the field of the arts have adequately proven, it is perhaps less the size of the grants than the form they take, the special encouragement they offer, that gives them their value and significance. Thus, the more than fifty years of awarding fellowships to creative individuals, especially the young, by the Guggenheim Foundation stand as an example of enlightened and meaningful foundation support.

It has been difficult for foundations to assess why some of their programs have permanent or at least enduring effect and others have not. This leads me to another reason why I would not wish to see our major foundations bring their arts programs to a halt. And that is simply that in the short time that the foundations have addressed themselves to the arts, they have proceeded pretty much by trial and error. I don't think they have yet reached their full potential in service to the arts.

In a way it's regrettable that the major foundations and the government discovered the arts almost at the same time. If the foundations had been given a real head start, they might have been able to carve out their role a little more sharply before public funding started moving in. As it was, they had hardly begun before they found themselves in competition, as it seemed, with the government.

I wish, for example, that the foundations had been able to develop a more coherent philosophy of support for music, an approach that would take into account just what is unique about music and its needs and also about its value. I wish they had had a clearer view of *why* they were supporting music, *how* they should go about giving that support, and just *what* it was that should be the real object of that support. Music was different from the fields in which the foundations had done most of their work over the years—science, health, international relations, education, fields in which research and support promised results. And so it was, I suppose, unavoidable that the foundations would reach back to the old idea of doing good works and began by treating music as an object of charity. This idea has been very hard to get rid of.

But music funding should not be considered a form of charity, a relief program either for performing organizations, or composers or even contemporary music itself. An object of charity is someone who is down and out, someone who inspires not your admiration, but your pity. Charitable donations are rarely intended to help down and outers find ways to improve their situation, and are generally guilt-appeasing substitutes for a solution.

As an example of foundation charity, let me cite the Ford Foundation's 1959 American Opera plan. Ford gave $950,000 to four major opera houses for the commissioning and production of eighteen new American operas during the next eight years. The composers were chosen by the administrators of the opera institutions. In what was an act of lack of faith, the foundation also agreed to reimburse the opera companies for the difference in box office take between their new American works and the standard works they might otherwise be giving. In effect, they subsidized empty seats. No one even thought of giving away free tickets to the operas. This program was doomed to fail right from its inception—and it did. None of these operas found its way into the repertory of an opera institution or student opera workshop. As Elliott Carter has put it so well, such acts of charity "tacitly imply the belief that American music will always be poor, but that it is a worthy act to help the poor."

Instead of feeling sorry for twentieth-century music and making the composers who write it and the performers who will agree to play it objects of charity, foundations should regard their efforts in behalf of composers and their music as a way of guaranteeing the continued benefits and enlightenment of contemporary musical thought and creation. Thus, no composer is ever in their debt for having been helped.

The continuing problem of *how* to go about funding music is brought into focus in the letter Henry Ford wrote when he resigned as a member of the Board of Trustees of the Ford Foundation recently. He wrote:

The Foundation has always prided itself on its emphasis on funding the experimental kind of effort—the new way that might lead to a significant breakthrough. Yet we stick with some programs for years and years—Office of the Arts being a prime example. Are we an ongoing funding agency or are we courageous backers of innovation. . . ?

The answer to Mr. Ford's question as far as music is concerned is that foundations have to be both ongoing funding agencies and courageous backers of innovation.

As Dwight MacDonald once pointed out, foundations don't like "steady pensioners." They don't like to get loaded up with future commitments. They like the idea of weaning a grantee after a certain point, of making him forage for himself.

Unfortunately for that point of view, music needs continuing subsidy. It will never be able to stand alone in the marketplace. Yet simply giving money every year to subsidize orchestras and opera houses, no matter what they do, is not the answer. Foundations rightly assess their role when they sense that their grants should lead to change. The point is that even long-term support does not necessarily have to be support of the status quo.

In science and medicine, foundations have been able to make grants that have helped bring about many a breakthrough. In the case of music, I am not sure that the foundations have clearly understood what might constitute a breakthrough. For many, the idea of giving a grant to any kind of so-called classical music organization seems innovative in itself. Many people honestly believe that the fact that we have far larger audiences for the music of Beethoven and Brahms and Verdi is in itself a tremendous breakthrough. Among some there persists the view that one can demonstrate progress simply by counting up the number of contemporary scores that a foundation has commissioned or that an orchestra has performed once. It should be understood that works that are played once and then dropped might as well be water under the bridge so far as any lasting effect is concerned. The extent to which we will ever experience a real breakthrough in music is directly proportionate to the number of twentieth-century scores that enter the repertory of our orchestras and opera houses. And I say twentieth-century scores rather then contemporary scores because works that enter the permanent repertory should properly be proven works, works that provide a frame of reference for the newer music. But our orchestras have very few twentieth-century classics in their repertory. Of the music written in the last forty years, perhaps only Bartok's *Concerto for Orchestra* is a repertory piece. There is much music by masters of our century who are no longer living, such as Debussy, Schoenberg, Berg, Webern, Stravinsky, Varèse, and others, that still is not in the repertory. Our orchestras and opera houses have drawn no closer to the twentieth century than they were in the early Sixties. Because our orchestras play occasional contemporary works without maintaining very many of their antecedents in the repertory, one gets the impression of visiting an art museum where only the treasures of past centuries and works of the latest recipients of Guggenheim fellowships are shown. No wonder audiences are bewildered. Would it help foundations to understand the kind of breakthrough that is required in music if they would think of their role not only as giving "seed money," but also paying for "cultivation"?

31

Closely related to the question of a breakthrough in music is the problem of deciding just *what* it is that is the real object of support in a foundation music program. To date, support has been given mainly to performing organizations, and secondly, although less frequently, to composers, but, as I will explain, not to twentieth-century music.

It has been estimated that the Ford Foundation has given nearly $1 billion to American orchestras. The most spectacular grant was the $80 million challenge or matching grant announced in 1966. These matching grants have been quite popular with government as well as foundations.

I like the idea of offering a challenge. But what I don't understand is why we should challenge orchestras and opera houses merely to raise money. Why can't we challenge them to do something else? Why not give money only on the condition that they build up the twentieth-century content of their repertory or forfeit the money they've been given? Confronted with such a choice, they would have to come to terms with their responsibilities as cultural institutions as well as custodians of music history. And who would dispute the fact that what our composers are doing in our midst will become the history of music of our time?

The problem with matching grants without any artistic conditions attached is that they reward performing groups for becoming good fund-raisers. If an orchestra can come up with matching funds by the deadline, they get their grant. It makes no difference what kind of programming they offer. It doesn't matter that in order to raise the kind of money that is required by the challenge, they are forced to make their programs all the more conservative.

If giving money to orchestras doesn't necessarily mean supporting twentieth-century music, neither does supporting composers mean supporting music. This may sound contradictory, but let's take a closer look at the situation.

The image of the contemporary composer as orphan has had great appeal for foundations. We want to be the good parents who bestow our affection upon the adopted child in the form of fellowships, prizes, and commissions in order that he may have the opportunity to produce musical works without interruption. And we feel that if we could keep him busy writing music we would not only help him individually, but also serve the cause of contemporary music.

And so the composer goes from premiere to premiere, quite dazzled by it all when he is young, but experiencing a strange sense of frustration as time goes on. He begins to wonder why it is that the orchestra that has recently commissioned a work from him wants to play a new piece of his when it has never or rarely performed any of his existing music. Or why, when he is almost commission-ridden, his music is still unknown as a whole even to audiences for contemporary music. Chicago knows one piece, and maybe Los Angeles or New York still another. If his music shows a growing and changing style, each of these audiences may have a rather different view of his work. He is also puzzled why his compositions should receive less recognition than his status as a composer.

What has happened is that, in our rush of good will, we have adopted the composer, but we have created a new orphan—the composer's music. Even at the moment the composer is applauded for his latest premiere, he knows that the work itself has very little likelihood of being played again, published, or recorded. He realizes that he has succumbed to the temptation of producing a quantity of music far beyond our society's willingness to absorb or nurture, a situation directly analagous to that of the world population. Stravinsky rightly pointed out that foundations have been buying up music the way the government buys up surplus corn.

What we need now is not more and more commissions, but a form of musical birth control. Instead of a proliferation of commissions, we need to support additional performances of already existing scores.

I have spent so much of my time talking about the first pair of steeds, the patrons, partly because talking about musical patronage necessarily involves talking about performers and composers and about music itself. But I would still like to talk briefly about performers and composers, about how the special nature of the situation they each find themselves in may have caused them to falter in their contribution to the progress of twentieth-century music.

Patrons probably would not have to concern themselves with applying leverage if orchestras and opera companies would emulate theater groups and dance companies. Theater and dance people have remained in touch with the work of living artists, and are always eager to perform serious new works. Joseph Papp, one of the country's most dynamic and creative theater directors, said, "Actors' theaters are dead theaters and good directing is never visible. Any theater to be alive has to be a writers' theater."

Can you imagine the head of one of our big opera companies saying, "Singers' opera is dead opera"? Or a big name symphony music directory saying, "Any concert hall to be alive must be a composers' hall"?

We hear so often that performers and composers have become alienated from each other or that performers have become alienated from contemporary music. I think that what has really been happening is that most of our "brand name" performers and their followers among young concert artists are becoming alienated from music. Not only contemporary music. All music. I don't think this is altogether the performer's fault. But it is a tendency that performers should guard against. It has a kind of circular cause. Because the same works are played over and over, the focus is on performance rather than on the music. But, also, because of the focus on performance, the same works are played over and over.

What we used to characterize as "the music business" has become a performance industry. The media-led cult of personality has played a large part in this development. It is the performer's face that appears on the cover of *Time* magazine. And so it follows that music is viewed as an extension of the personality of the performer. Public television recently offered us Sir Georg Solti as high culture's answer to John Travolta. At least, that was the implication of the title *Symphony Night Fever*, given to a series of three Chicago Symphony television specials aired in January. It should not be surprising that performers and conductors start viewing things this way, too, that they start thinking of music as vehicles for their ego trips.

Of course, artists have always had a good deal of ego strength, but it is one thing to feel that you achieve greatness as an interpreter insofar as you realize the composer's intentions. It's quite another thing to see a musical work primarily as a vehicle for your performance. It's one thing to want to share the excitement you feel about a musical work, to want to give pleasure. It's another thing to want the audience to remember the details of your performance rather than the impact of the music. The difference is the difference between character and personality.

When personality is king, then being successful simply means having a reputation as a winner, as someone who comes out ahead of the competition. Our most celebrated conductors and performers are the only ones who have the power to expand and enrich our musical culture by adding to the repertory, to illuminate music for their audiences through coherent programming. Unfortunately, they no longer view power as something that carries with it responsibilities and a sense of cultural mission.

We must not forget that the stakes are high in the performance industry. There is much fame to be earned and much money to be made, and there is tremendous competition for both. Performers no long pit themselves against a musical task or a musical problem demanding solution. Instead, they pit themselves against other performers. Because of this, the musical works themselves must be familiar. Viewed this way, musical works are like the school figures used in ice-skating competitions. They are played less because they are interesting in themselves than because they provide a way to rank the performers. This is a harsh comparison. But as our performers keep playing the same fifty famous pieces—as Virgil Thomson called them—over and over again, it's hard not to feel that they are just tracing figure 8's into the ice. The significance of a concert seems to be whether so-and-so's figure 8 wasn't just a little more graceful or more sweeping or bolder than so-and-so's. Certainly, critics spend nearly all their time reviewing performance rather than music. And the audience seems fascinated by playing this game, too.

There are, however, some people in concert audiences who grow impatient with this kind of fascination with comparative performance. They think that every performance they hear of the Beethoven *Ninth Symphony* is great just because the work is great. This may be a naive view, but at least, these people are still able to focus on music itself. They seek a musical experience and get it.

But, for the most part, our concert audiences are part of a society that is obsessed with the virtuoso aspects of performance, that worships performers and conductors as culture heroes, that is impressed by the proliferation of organized musical life, yet deaf to composition as the primary source of musical experience.

What happens to composers living in a world where works of music have lost their value? Where the music of the past lies in bondage to performance? Where most of the music of the present dies in the first performance, if it is performed at all?

Ned Rorem once wrote that "Doers and makers move in quite separate . . . orbits. Players face out, composers, in." I'm sure that this is true. As I have suggested, there are times when it seems to me that players face out—toward the public and away from music. But it is equally true that composers face in—away from the public and toward their own world of music.

Composers do not choose isolation, but rather have it thrust upon them. If our composers have often preferred not to view their musical offerings as vehicles of emotional communication, one reason may be the one that painter Robert Motherwell has suggested: that as members of our society as a whole, composers, along with other artists, have shared in that society's decreasing capacity for giving and receiving passion.

If some of our composers have allowed the cerebral structure of their music to be dominant, they may have done so partly because as members of university communities, they live in an environment where intellect is valued highly. It is important to stress that intellectualism has been both an advantage and a disadvantage for American music. As the composer Fred Lerdahl has pointed out, American composers, by being more "academic" than their European counterparts, have been less susceptible to "cheap effects and fashion-mongering." At the same time, he added that their music has sometimes shown a "loss in immediacy, boldness, and brilliance."

If our composers have increasingly become composers' composers rather than creators for the public at large, they have often done so because their colleagues seem to be the only people who are still excited about music as an on-going art form.

One could list many more factors than these that have brought about the isolation of our composers. The causes are legion. One further cause might even be one that Pierre Boulez has suggested, that composers' ideas today are more advanced than the materials they are working in, that these ideas will not develop fully until composers have instruments that are capable of fully realizing their musical thoughts and visions. As an analogy, Boulez cites developments in the field of architecture. "So long as it was confined to wood and stone," Boulez said, "architecture at the end of the nineteenth century seemed to have come to a dead end, seemed able only to imitate the past. Hence all the pseudo-Renaissance, pseudo-Greek buildings. Once concrete, glass, and steel became available, they imposed new laws of construction that are implicit in the material. It was simply not possible to make a Gothic capital with them." There is hope that the technological advances in instruments and exploration of new sound dimensions and sound environments that Boulez and his colleagues at IRCAM (the Musical Research Institute in Paris) are investigating will result in a universal musical vocabulary that will ultimately bridge the present gap between the composer's language of expression and the sensibilities of a sophisticated audience.

I am inclined to agree with Varèse, who once said, "Contrary to general belief, an artist is never ahead of time, but most people are far behind theirs." Varèse's comment was recently echoed and clarified by Andrew Porter writing in *The New Yorker*: "To the charge that many composers are out of touch with the public can be added another: that the public is out of touch with many of its best composers."

The point here is that the public is out of touch not just with advanced musical experimentation; that could be expected in any era. No, the public and most performers are out of touch with the twentiety-century classics—works of proven substance and great beauty. With twenty years yet to go, our century has already produced a body of music that would be the pride of any century. I can easily name twelve great twentieth-century masters from among composers who are already dead—Debussy, Mahler, Strauss, Ravel, Stravinsky, Bartok, Schoenberg, Berg, Webern, Varèse, Ives, Hindemith. As I live in a society that believes that only dead composers are good composers, I will not even attempt to name the important composers who are still living.

I am convinced that our century will eventually prove to be one of the great musical centuries. Our choices as performers, patrons, and listeners seem to me to be equally clear. Either we award ourselves the privilege of coming to know the great musical creations of our own century, or we leave these works to be discovered by future generations.

If we choose to ignore what is happening in our midst, it is exclusively our loss. For there is no doubt that twentieth-century music will complete her journey to the twenty-first century. She may arrive, unheralded, without the full panoply that befits her rank. Indeed, she may have to be sneaked over the border by a small band of devoted admirers. But, in any case, she will arrive.

A Musical Utopia

Originally presented as an intermission talk at a concert in the series "Music New to New York"
on January 12, 1981, this paper was then entitled "A Community of Musicians in Utopia."
It was printed in the Musical America *section of* High Fidelity / Musical America *(v. 31,*
no. 12, pp. 18-20) in December, 1981, with the title given here.

One evening a while ago, I chanced to pick up a copy of Berlioz's *Evenings with the Orchestra*. I was intrigued by a comment on the back cover of the book, about Berlioz's imaginary musical realm called Euphonia. The comment, by an unidentified reviewer, was this:

> Contrary to most utopias, Euphonia is a comic daydream never to be desired in reality.

After I had read what Berlioz had written about Euphonia, I was puzzled by the reviewer's remark. Did Berlioz really think of Euphonia as undesirable? Euphonia struck *me* as clearly utopian, at least in its depiction of a flourishing musical milieu. (As to such details as the composer/lover on a rose-strewn couch, wanting to end his life because he has achieved the perfect mating with a singer of gorgeous voice, great beauty, and musical intelligence of the highest degree—of that and similar fantasies, I shall venture no opinion.)

But take, for example, Euphonia's rule that concert audiences are to be chosen strictly on the basis of musical culture and sophistication. Surely one would call that utopian.

Or consider the approach that orchestras in Euphonia bring to a new score. "When some important new work is to be performed," writes Berlioz, "each part is studied separately for three or four days." Together, in rehearsals, the musicians work first for literal exactitude, next for broad nuances. And they don't stop there. They go on to work on subtleties of style and expression. Only after all this has been accomplished does the ensemble receive the composer's criticism. Berlioz writes:

> The composer has been listening from the upper part of the amphitheater which the public will occupy; and . . . when he is sure that nothing remains but to communicate to it the vital nuances that he feels and can impart better than anyone else, the moment has come for him to become a performer himself. He climbs the podium to conduct.

Surely this is utopian. But how might a musical utopia of Berlioz's time differ from one that *I*, for example, might envision? Could it be that what Berlioz intended to represent seems utopian to me because, in our time, we lack what Berlioz could take for granted: a vital musical culture?

I had not resolved this issue by bedtime. Not surprisingly, that night I had a dream in which it seemed that I had been transported to Euphonia. Yet my Euphonia was different from Berlioz's. It was like our present world—but it was not the world we know.

Let me tell you about my dream. I found myself in a meadow surrounded by woodlands, not unlike the grounds at Tanglewood. I could hear an orchestra tuning up. Among the scales and the sounds of random tuning, I caught fragments of Schoenberg and Stravinsky, as well as Wieniawsky and Brahms.

A friendly man came toward me and told me that I was in Euphonia. We walked toward an open structure— a kind of music shed—where an orchestra was beginning to rehearse. The performers looked very young to me, and there was a radiance in their faces that suggested more than mere youth. When I asked my guide about this, he assured me that all ages of performers, composers, and listeners were welcome in Euphonia. "Maybe our life here keeps people looking young," he said. "But why not ask a performer?"

He introduced me to a violinist, a soloist who was waiting to rehearse a concerto. "Mr. Fromm is amazed that you performers all look so happy," my guide said.

The violinist smiled. "Of course I can only speak for myself," he responded. "But in the pre-Euphonia days, I found myself getting bored. I played music for the wrong reasons. I performed particular works because I had been taught that I *should* play them, to prove that I *could* play them, I guess—not because they needed to be performed. There were plenty of competent performers, and we were all playing the same repertoire, from the late 18th and 19th centuries. We were not colleagues, but competitors, all struggling for fame. The key was publicity. If you could get good notices and make the public more aware of you than the others, you had arrived."

"Shortly before Euphonia came into being," the violinist answered, "I got involved in contemporary music. And I discovered a new purpose. I found it more satisfying to play music in order that the music be heard, than to strive to prove my own virtuosity. Then I noticed that the same feeling extended to older scores. The old warhorses don't automatically get played in Euphonia—they have to take their chances along with all the works, old and new. When I play one of them, I do it because I like it, and think it should be heard. This sense of purpose, a feeling that music is played because it should be heard, also extends to orchestra musicians. If they know that they are participating in the only live performance of Beethoven's Ninth Symphony in a decade, they all play with an exalted degree of artistry."

The violinist went onstage to rehearse, and it fell to my guide to explain how this strange, new world had come into being. "Euphonia's founding was an attempt to realize certain ideals of music making," he said, "but also in part a reaction against what its founders believed were musical abuses, back in the pre-Euphonia world.

"The founders believed that music making had become a purely visual reading skill. This was made explicit by one of Euphonia's founders back in 1977. Let me read from a pamphlet I always carry with me:

> Musicians have developed the art of reading pitches (and the more familiar rhythms) to such a high level of technical competence that we are in immi-

nent danger of no longer needing our ears—except for the crudest of note repairs. We do it all with our eyes whilst our ears gradually atrophy from disuse. We have accomplished the ultimate musical ingenuity . . . we have learned to transform musical performing into a reading/visual skill, eliminating the very thing for which music exists; hearing, aural perception and aural sensitivity.

"The founders felt that by requiring composers to teach their music to performers by ear, and by requiring players to memorize already existing scores, they could help all musicians recover the use of their ears. This had a considerable effect on the relationship between composers and performers, many of whom, in the pre-Euphonia days, simply did not inhabit the same world. Once it became clear that musicians had regained the use of their ears, of course, the rule by which scores had to be memorized was no longer enforced.

"And works-in-progress sessions have also brought composers and performers into closer contact. Composers here have the option to sign up for the time of whatever ensemble they are writing for—even a complete opera company. The cooperating ensembles are not required to polish their performances of these unfinished works; a rough version is sufficient to give the composer a validation of what he heard when he put his notes on paper. This procedure has given the performers a new feeling of involvement. One player told me, 'You have no idea what it's like to work with a composer, to know that the way you play his notes may affect what he writes.' "

"But how," I wondered, "do you get these groups—especially big orchestras and opera ensembles—to use rehearsal time to go through works-in-progress? I remember a time when orchestras and opera companies would not perform new works even after they had been completed."

"It is greatly to the performing ensemble's advantage to do this—artistically as well as financially," said my guide. "We have a new system of grant-giving. In pre-Euphonia days, as you recall, grants did not challenge musical organizations to change their practice of glutting us with Romantic and post–Romantic music. Most grants in those days had no purpose other than to spur administrators to more aggressive fund-raising. To larger organizations, fund-raising had become an end in itself, and it got in the way of artistic standards and integrity.

"But in Euphonia, the grants reward performers for making contributions to a continuing, growing musical culture—for adding new or recent works to their permanent repertoires, for imaginative programming, for rehearsing works-in-progress, for giving the works they perform adequate rehearsal, and for innovative experiments in bringing music to children.

"By the way," my guide continued, "you may be particularly interested to know that in Euphonia, composers are not directly commissioned. The grants given to performers require them to play a certain number of recent scores. The performers (or, in the cases of larger ensembles, the music directors) decide whether to perform an existing work by a contemporary composer, or to commission a new piece. It has turned out that performers now play more commissioned works *and* more works of the early 20th century than ever—the ratio between first, second, and even tenth performances has changed drastically. You yourself raised this issue in pre-Euphonia days."

Reading again from that worn pamphlet, my guide quoted me to myself:

> Even at the moment the composer is applauded for his latest premiere, he knows that the work itself has very little likelihood of being played again, published, or recorded. He realizes that he has succumbed to the temptation of producing a quantity of music far beyond our society's willingness to absorb or nurture, a situation directly analagous to that of the world population. . . . What we need now is not more and more commissions, but a form of musical birth control. Instead of a proliferation of commissions, we need to support additional performances of already existing scores.

"Another advantage of leaving the commissioning to the discretion of the performer," my guide explained, "is that the composer is obliged to write something that someone would want to perform. Some people used to worry that composers who wrote for performers would produce shallow, virtuoso music. Others were concerned that composers might attempt to ensure performances by writing music that was easy to learn. But performers who advocate the music of a particular composer are making investments of time and risking their reputations. Therefore, they tend to select good works."

A composer was approaching us. My guide suggested that we ask her how she felt about the new priorities.

"I don't know that any of us writes *for* performers directly," she said. "We still write for ourselves, believing that if our music has meaning to us, it must have meaning to some others. What is different is that there is no longer quite the obsession with masterpieces that there once was. Performers try, no doubt, to choose music they like, but they have that imperturbable faith that, sooner or later, what is important will emerge."

"What about the audiences?" I asked.

"It may be hard to believe," the composer said, "but listeners continue to be drawn to music that is played with deep commitment and conviction."

"Please," I said, "exactly when and where is Euphonia? Is this a prophecy? If we wait long enough, will Euphonia come to be?"

But my guide had faded from view.

When I woke up, I pondered my dream. Could it be called an utopian vision? Dreams rarely offer a comprehensive experience, but only fragments of a vision. And I am still not sure whether any utopian vision is meant to embody ideals that are desirable in themselves, or whether it satirizes unacceptable realities. In Jonathan Swift's *Gulliver's Travels,* the kingdom of the Houyhnhnms, those rational and benign horses, had no place for human conduct and emotion, and could not serve as a substitute for our world. So, too, Euphonia is too perfect for human habitation.

Euphonia, then, can never really exist. But there is a sense in which the realm has a fleeting presence. Moments of Euphonia exist at Tanglewood and some other special places across the country. Euphonia exists wherever composers and performers join together to recognize their interdependence, and, instead of competing, work together toward shared artistic goals. Euphonia exists when musicians are joined by poets, writers, painters, sculptors, dancers, and other members of the cultural community—and by the small but growing group of listeners who believe that no art can be more important to them than the art that is created in their own time. Euphonia, Berlioz's vision of a utopian community of musicians, will always underlie our hopes for the coming of a musical culture in which serious artistry is encouraged, and in which music flourishes as a living art.

Creative Women in Music:
A Historical Perspective

This address was presented on February 3, 1986, at Tulane University in New Orleans as part of "Vivace—A Contemporary Music Festival."

I am happy to have been invited to take part in so festive and auspicious an occasion, an occasion three times over, it seems to me.

First, and most eminently, we are here this week to celebrate the fiftieth anniversary of the founding of the New Orleans Symphony. Others have had and will have much to say about the Symphony's history and progress. But allow me to congratulate Maestro Maxim Shostakovich on his appointment as Music Director. A musician of his stature will assure the continued pre-eminence of the Orchestra at home and on the national music scene.

Second, this week is a forward-looking occasion as well as a commemoration because a major orchestra and a major university are joined in presenting a festival of contemporary music.

What makes this occasion truly auspicious, moreover, is that two of the composers whose works are being performed this week are women—Deborah Drattell and Faye-Ellen Silverman. According to the Orchestra's public relations department, the work of only one other woman composer has ever been played by the New Orleans Symphony—Thea Musgrave in 1975, the year designated by the United Nations as the International Women's Year.

I have some familiarity with the music of both Ms. Drattell and Ms. Silverman. Both are recipients of Fromm Foundation commissions. Up to the present time, the Fromm Foundation has commissioned twelve works by women composers, but it is symptomatic of our male-oriented culture that it took us until 1970 to award a commission to a woman.

Ms. Drattell's *Spirits of the Dead* will be heard in Friday's concert. Like her work for chorus and orchestra, *The Tell-Tale Heart,* which was premiered last month by the New Orleans Symphony, *Spirits of the Dead* is based on the writing of Edgar Allan Poe. Ms. Drattell's Fromm Foundation commission was a setting of still another work by Poe, a poem called "Alone," and was first performed in 1984 by the Contemporary Chamber Players of the University of Chicago under the direction of Ralph Shapey. Her fascination with the writings of Edgar Allan Poe finds poetic expression in her music. Ms. Drattell, who studied both composition and conducting with Ralph Shapey, no doubt was also inspired by him to create a contemporary music ensemble of her own. She once told me that Ralph Shapey often teased her about wanting to be the female Ralph Shapey. If one adds the success of her ensemble, *First Monday Contemporary Chamber Ensemble,* and the organizational skill that has made this week possible, to her talent as a composer, it appears that the day may come when young male composer-conductors may feel honored to be known as male Deborah Drattells.

Our search for emerging composers of the younger generation led the Fromm Foundation to the music of Faye-Ellen Silverman. We became familiar with her music in the beginning of 1985, and since we found her to be an extraordinarily gifted composer still to be discovered, we have supported her career by putting her music on the programs of concerts which we have sponsored. We also commissioned her to write a work for chamber ensemble for the Monday Evening Concerts in Los Angeles. The piece, *Passing Fancies,* will be premiered in Los Angeles on February 17th. Her orchestral work, *Winds and Sines,* which won the Indiana State University's Orchestral Composition Contest in 1982, will be heard Thursday evening. It is dedicated to the composer and pioneer of electronic music, Vladimir Ussachevsky, and draws on sound materials from the two areas which have fascinated Ussachevsky: the desert lands of Utah, particularly desert winds, and the sounds of electronic music.

So, with the Orchestra's anniversary and the performance of several works by contemporary composers, including some by women, we do have a variety of milestones to celebrate.

Although I am reluctant to say anything that would dampen the enthusiasm of anyone here tonight, yet I must confess that, in some ways, this week is more of an occasion than I would wish it to be.

I wish, for one thing, that first performances of new musical works were so much a part of orchestra programming by now that they would pass almost unnoticed unless a work of singular merit came along. Such a work would then be routinely scheduled for repeat performances in future seasons and, if it continued to be viewed favorably, it would eventually become part of the orchestra's permanent repertory.

More particularly, I wish that music written by contemporary female composers were played by orchestras with even a quarter of the frequency that music by contemporary male composers is performed. Both as a male and as an active member of the musical community, I am embarrassed that—this late in the 20th century—a performance by an orchestra of a work by a female composer is still an uncommon event. The music of all contemporary composers has been so neglected by the musical establishment that it is difficult to imagine that women composers can be in a worse plight than their male colleagues. Nevertheless, even a very high number of programs put on by organizations devoted to performing contemporary music contain no works by women. And, of course, orchestral music and operas by women composers of the past have so far been completely lost to us.

I am embarrassed that—this late in the 20th century—women composers are still being announced as the first to do this and the first to do that. Yet we keep hearing such announcements. In 1983 the Pulitizer Prize in music was awarded for the first time to a woman—Ellen Taafe Zwilich—for her *Three Movements for Orchestra—Symphony No. 1.* Ms. Zwilich was also the first woman to receive a doctorate in music composition from the Juilliard School of Music. That was as recently as 1975. It is incredible to me that such a milestone could come that late. Back in 1913, when she was only 19, Lili Boulanger was the first woman to win the *Grand Prix de Rome*, but she won it anonymously. Five years later, she submitted another work, this time under her own name, and was not even allowed to compete. The competition, she was told, was restricted to males under 30.

I am embarrassed that even though the *International Encyclopedia of Women Composers*, which came out in 1981, lists over 5,000 women who are known to have composed music, most of us would find it difficult to list even a few names of women composers from either the present or the past. How many of you are able to think offhand of more than five names in addition to the two female composers whose works are being performed this week? If it were not for the limited scope of this address, I would have to go back far in history or at least begin in the 11th century when Abbess Hildegardis of Bingen wrote music of enduring value. Some of her compositions are preserved in contemporary recordings.

Most music lovers, when pressed to name women composers of the past, have an inkling that Robert Schumann's wife Clara wrote some music. And some may also have heard that Fanny Mendelssohn, the sister of Felix Mendelssohn, was a published composer, but very few people could name such composers as:

Germaine Tailleferre, who along with Poulenc, Honneger, Milhaud, Auric and Durey, was one of the famous group of six composers known as *Les Six* in Paris in the 1920s;

Dame Ethel Smyth, a British opera composer whose early compositions were so admired by Brahms that he refused to believe that they were written by a woman, and whose operas were performed in Germany and England, and, one of them, in 1903, at the Metropolitan;

Amy Cheney Beach, an American composer who lived in Boston in the late 1800s, whose *Gaelic Symphony* was the first symphony written by an American woman composer and was performed not only by the Boston Symphony Orchestra in 1896, but also by the Philadelphia Orchestra and the Chicago Symphony;

Ruth Crawford Seeger, who was a major artist in the American modernist movement. She was an active member of the avant-garde in the late '20s and early '30s, and is now recognized as one of the important and innovative composers of our century.

What's more, many contemporary women composers have *themselves* been unaware of the existence of other women composers, especially those from the past, until quite recently. One contemporary composer, Emma Lou Diemer, recently told an interviewer, "I can remember well that a few years ago the only names of women composers that I knew were Clara Schumann and myself." Another contemporary composer, Priscilla McLean, has written, "I was brought up to believe that all composers were men."

Small wonder that Ms. McLean was given that impression, for as late as the 1975 edition, *Webster's American Biographies,* which included 3,000 significant Americans, did not mention one American woman composer.

Once, several years ago, I was given an award by Mu Phi Epsilon. I felt guilty about receiving an award from a woman's music sorority. I thought of myself as some sort of interloper, encroaching on an honor that might have gone to a musically creative woman. I wasn't a woman. I wasn't even a composer. And so I decided to accept on behalf of the women composers who had received Fromm Foundation commissions. Tonight, if you will allow me to present myself as a male feminist, I wish to speak on behalf of the neglected women composers of the past and the emerging women composers of the present. From time to time I will let them speak for themselves in their own words because they have had enlightening comments to make on the plight of women composers.

I would like to speak first about the obstacles that have prevented women from becoming recognized composers.

The primary obstacle has been lack of opportunity.

The question has often been asked, "Why when there have been great women novelists, have there not been eminent women composers?" Writing great novels can be a relatively homebound craft, as the works of Jane Austen and the Bronte sisters bear witness. Musical composition is not a self-taught language, but rather an extremely complicated craft that requires a host of learned skills. Women generally have been denied the necessary resources for learning these skills.

Since the 18th century a small dose of music has been considered a female adornment. Earlier, in Renaissance times, both gentlemen and ladies were expected to develop some little proficiency in the arts. Later, as the middle class and their workaday world became dominant, men abandoned these leisure diversions and left them to women as their exclusive property.

However, serious professional preparation for music has traditionally been the exclusive province of males. In the great German conservatories, even in the very late 19th century, women could enroll in a course in elementary harmony, but they were not allowed to take counterpoint.

Women have also traditionally been kept from performing in contexts that make a difference for budding composers. During the long centuries in which music exclusively served the Church, choir boys who took an interest in music could steep their minds in the harmonies and contrapuntal intricacies of the music they sang. They could pay attention to the effects to be obtained from the organ and observe what the choir master did to train the choir. Choir girls were nonexistent in the man's world of the Church.

The symphony orchestra, another musical context in which composers learn much about their craft, has also been a man's world. Even today, there are not as many women in our major orchestras as there should be. I hasten to say that the New Orleans Symphony has had a better record in this regard than most others. The reasons that have been given for not allowing women in orchestras are incredible:

In the early part of this century, an eastern seaboard music critic defended the exclusion of women from orchestras by asking what he thought were rhetorical questions:

"Can a conductor enforce discipline among the women as well as he can among the men, or will they have recourse to the defense of tears when the hard-hearted one addresses the instrumental body in a merciless rebuke? Can women endure the severe strain of long and repeated rehearsal?"

Orchestras first allowed women to enter their ranks as harpists. There was apparently something muselike about a woman who played the harp. Later, a few women violinists were allowed into the men's orchestras. Women cellists were considered vulgar for a long time, and even as late as the 1930s it was not really acceptable for women to blow horns of any kind—because horn-blowing distorted their pretty faces—or to play drums; playing drums required an unseemly display of athleticism. And for a woman to play the bull fiddle—well, the appellation *bull fiddle* tells its own story.

In the 1940s there was *still* concern that women would have a disruptive influence on the men in the orchestra. One of Sir Thomas Beecham's famous remarks at the time expressed this attitude. Said Sir Thomas, "If the ladies are ill-favored, the men do not wish to play next to them, and if they are well-favored, they cannot."

A second obstacle has been the role that women have been expected to play in society. They were wives and mothers with households to run and husbands to make life easy for. Many musical women were the daughters or sisters or wives of composers whose work they supported. Clara Schumann, for example, was a crucial force in the promotion of the music of her husband, Robert. Women who had managed to learn how to compose music as a result of growing up in musical families were permitted to do it only if the composing did not get in the way of what was perceived as their primary duties.

When, for example, in 1837, Fanny Mendelssohn—by this time married to Wilhelm Hensel and the mother of a young son—had had one song published and had expressed an interest in having some of her other compositions published, her brother Felix wrote with great vehemence to their mother as follows:

> . . . You write to me about Fanny's new compositions, and say that I ought to persuade her to publish them. . . . I cannot, because this is contrary to my views and convictions. . . . From my knowledge of Fanny, I should say that she has neither inclination nor vocation for authorship. She is too much all that a woman ought to be for this. She regulates her house, and neither thinks of the public nor of the musical world, nor even of music at all, until her first duties are fulfilled. Publishing would only disturb her in these, and I cannot say I approve of it.

Fanny Mendelssohn, accordingly, put off publishing any more of her songs and piano pieces for many years. Finally the bids of two rival publishers inspired her to publish them, and in the glow of this recognition she wrote a work of larger scale, her Piano Trio in D Minor. She died a short time after writing the Trio, but her last diary entries suggest that she wanted to go on to compose music of larger scope.

Another obstacle facing the would-be women composers has been the persistent theory that even if women had had the opportunity to learn what they needed to know to become composers, they would have failed to do so because of some defect in their nature. I'll give you just a few examples of statements reflecting variations on this theory in chronological order so that you will be able to follow the March of Progress in the thinking about the nature of a woman's mind and psychology.

In 1898 George Upton, a Chicago music critic, explained that a woman is unable to write great music because she cannot control her emotions sufficiently to give artistic expression to them as, in Upton's view, a man can. Upton's proof for his theory was simply that women have failed to write great music in the past.

Here's a woman, Marian Cox, definitely not a composer, writing in the Chicago Tribune in 1920: If I paraphrase what she wrote, you won't believe it, so let me quote her directly: "Music is, biologically, a function of the male, in the game of sex, man's most splendiferous gift is to charm, subdue and conquer an audience, a woman or an enemy. The musician's temperament is martial or amorous, his gift aggressive in its need of something to affect and to act upon. Woman thus becomes the natural object of music and musicians, and her temperament equips her to be the great music lover. . . . " She goes on, but I think you've heard enough.

In 1940 psychologist Carl E. Seashore explained elaborately that women were equal to men in musical talent, in intelligence, even in opportunities for musical education. The reason that women did not become great composers was that a woman's fundamental urge was different from a man's. Woman's fundamental urge, said Seashore, is to be beautiful, loved, and adored as a person; man's urge is to provide and achieve in a career.

As recently as 1973, the psychologist Grace Rubin-Rabson stated that there are innate qualities that great composers need that women lack. In her view, composers need to have an investigative, exploratory turn of mind, a messianic vision of their work, and obsessive dedication. Her proof that women lack these qualities is that while baby male monkeys run, fight, and explore, baby female monkeys sit and watch. As far as I can tell, the requirements that Ms. Rubin-Rabson has listed also keep many men from becoming great composers. And I do not know any monkeys, male or female, who have become composers, let alone great composers.

Another obstacle that women composers have had to face, one that would be more amusing if it were not so pathetic, is the kind of mental gymnastics engaged in by those who insisted on analyzing music *itself* in terms of masculine and feminine traits. As Carol Neuls-Bates has characterized this analysis in her book *Women in Music,* "Feminine music was by definition graceful and delicate, full of melody, and restricted to the smaller forms of songs and piano music. Masculine music, by contrast, was powerful in effect and intellectually rigorous in harmony, counterpoint and other structural logic. Symphonies, operas and similarly large-scaled works lay in the realm of masculine music." Analyzing music this way allowed reviewers to present the virtues and defects in a musical work by a woman as the inevitable result of her gender, as in the following excerpts from turn-of-the-century reviews of music by women:

From a review of Amy Beach's *Gaelic Symphony:* "Occasionally the music is noisy rather than sonorous. Here Mrs. Beach is entirely feminine. A woman who writes for orchestra thinks, 'I must be virile at any cost.' "

And from another review of the same work: "What she [Mrs. Beach] says in her work has been said a thousand times before, and better said, yet there is no gainsaying her industry, her gift for melody . . . and her lack of logic. Contrapuntally she is not strong. Of grace and delicacy there are evidences in the Siciliana, and there she is at her best, but yet a woman."

And then from a review of an opera by the English composer Ethel Smyth: "Not as the music of a woman should Miss Smyth's score be judged. She thinks in masculine style, broad and virile. She has fully mastered the modern orchestral mode. Her melodic vein is pronounced. Its contours are bold and straight."

When these theorists tried to analyze the music of the great male composers in terms of masculine and feminine traits, they ran into trouble. The works of Bach, Mozart, Haydn and even Beethoven were found to have feminine qualities such as lyric sweetness, melting adagios, neurotic melancholy, subjective nervous motion, and, in the case of Mozart, a twittering gush of notes!

Lest you think that analyzing music in terms of masculine and femine traits is an attitude safely buried in the past, listen to what contemporary composer Priscilla McLean has to tell about two quite recent experiences:

Reports Ms. McLean: "One noted Midwestern orchestral conductor told me he believed that there definitely was a 'woman's music,' which was delicate, soft, unctuous in harmonies, organic in form, and so on. I answered by telling him that he had exactly described the music of Debussy, and how did he account for that?

"Another conversation took place after a two-piano piece of mine called *Interplanes* was played on the radio. Without knowing that I had written the work, a male composer friend of mine who had been researching contemporary music for years remarked that here was a definitely masculine work—strong, forceful, driving, dissonant, and so on—and was astounded to hear that the work was mine."

In an article called *Ladies Music*, Ned Rorem said that music is the most sexless of the arts, and I am inclined to agree. But regardless, the presence now of a great variety of styles of both men and women may finally drive the notion of masculine and feminine traits in music into the ground.

Another obstacle that women who have managed to compose music have faced and are still facing is a strong tendency for the sword of music criticism against music by women to be double-edged. One edge of the sword is music criticism that patronizes and insults women composers by not taking their work seriously and by substituting gallantry for real evaluation. The other edge of the sword is music criticism that judges music by women more harshly than music by men. A poor or mediocre score by a man is just that; it is not viewed as evidence that all men should immediately cease composing. But a poor or mediocre score by a woman has been and still is often offered as proof that women should not even attempt to compose.

So far I have been talking about the external obstacles that have kept women from becoming composers—lack of opportunity, the role in society that women have been expected to play, notions about the nature of a woman's mind and psychology, notions about the nature of music, the way in which critical standards have been applied against music by women.

The most imposing barrier of all, however, may be the barrier that has developed in the woman composer's mind, the psychological barrier that results from the process of internalizing cultural attitudes. Germaine Greer, in her splendid book about the historical struggle of women painters, *The Obstacle Race*, has commented brilliantly on the nature of the psychological obstacles that women artists face. I would like to quote what she says, paraphrasing her words slightly to apply them to women composers:

Greer says, "All women are tortured by contradictory pressures, but none more so than the female artist. . . . A woman knows that she is to be womanly and she also knows that for a musical composition to be womanish is contemptible. The choices are before her: to deny her sex, which is an immensely costly proceeding in terms of psychic energy, or to accept her sex and with it second place. . . . For all artists, the problem is one of finding one's own authenticity, or speaking in a language . . . that is essentially one's own, but if one's self-image is dictated by one's relations to others and all one's activities are other-directed, it is simply not possible to find one's own voice."

It is easy to laugh at what we can now easily recognize as misguided notions of the past. But as I have tried to suggest here and there, many of the old attitudes about women and composing still influence us today—although they are usually expressed in more subtle ways or not directly expressed at all.

There has, of course, been tremendous improvement in the lot of the women composer, although there is much room for further progress.

Two-thirds of the women composers listed in the *International Encyclopedia of Women Composers* that I mentioned earlier are living composers.

A recent Schwann catalog lists some 1,300 composers. Only 32 of them—2.4 percent—are women composers, but 85 percent of those 32 are contemporary women, and 65 percent contemporary American women.

When in 1974 the Fromm Foundation asked members of the musical community around the country to list musical works written in the last forty years by American composers that had been neglected, 30 of the 686 composers whose works were mentioned were women. That's 4.5 percent. This may be a strange example of progress, but statistically speaking, awareness of women as neglected composers ranks higher than acknowledgment of women composers' works by the recording industry.

More than a dozen orchestras around the country included premieres of works by women composers in their programming last season.

Perhaps such organizations as the League of Women Composers, which was formed in 1975, have a potentially important role to play in furthering music by women. In addition to sponsoring concerts of women's music and seminars about women's music, it can challenge allocations of public funds from which women are excluded. For example, orchestras that fail to program works by women would not receive grants from the National Endowment for the Arts. Private foundations that award grants and commissions exclusively to men could have their tax-exempt status challenged.

Among women composers today there is, however, considerable controversy about the role of the League of Women Composers and about the issue of separatism versus integration of music by women. This issue, simply stated, is: Will special concerts devoted to women's music help integrate that music into the mainstream of musical culture or will such separatism become a substitute for integration? There are significant numbers of women composers on both sides of this issue and for good reason. The issue has all the earmarks of a dilemma.

The only way I can see to resolve the issue is to take a separatist approach to music by women composers of the past and an integrative approach to the music women are writing in the present.

In studying the music by women of the past, we actually need to apply the principles that lie behind separatism. We need first of all to defer the question of value—at least temporarily. That is, we need to learn as much as possible about the music women have written in the past without worrying about whether or not it has enduring merit.

We need to ask questions such as, What music by women of the past still exists? What does it show us about women's struggles to become composers? In other words, we need to find the music, perform it in special concerts, get special funding to record it, hold seminars on it, write books about it, but, most of all, integrate important works by women into the standard repertory.

Why is it so important to exhume this neglected music?

One reason is that present-day women composers need to be given a sense of their own tradition. Let me quote another composer, Annea Lockwood, originally from New Zealand, now in New York, who speaks about how it feels to grow up without any awareness of a tradition of women composers into which she could fit.

"I slowly became aware of the preponderance of male figures in the cultural world. I was educated solely by men once I'd reached the university level, with the exception of my piano teacher. . . . Had I had close contact with a woman composer during those years, I would have become aware of the cultural imbalance much sooner and it might have enabled me to see what I thought were merely personal problems in a truer and broader context. . . . As for the benefits of growing up learning about the women musicians and composers of earlier periods, they were so totally absent from texts and consideration that I can't fathom the extent of the difference it would have made having their names and work before me."

Another reason for digging up music by women composers of the past is that there may be some musical treats in store for us. Since the 1880s at least some music reviewers have been announcing that women composers are coming into their own. In fact, this sort of announcement has formed a kind of counterpoint against the series of statements we looked at before, the statements that try to explain why women aren't great composers. Scholars are turning up names of women composers who have had some acclaim in their day and who have published works that are still in existence. Some of the music that has been neglected deserves to be neglected, whether it is written by men or women. But there will inevitably be scores that will repay hearing.

Our responsibility to women composers of the present is very different from our responsibility to those of the past. We ought not to segregate the music of women in ghetto concerts but to play it on regular programs as it is being done here this week. I don't think we do women composers of today a service by offering them a handicap as if they were golfers who hit way over par. To do so is to continue to patronize them. We need to evaluate contemporary women composers by the same standards that apply to male composers.

The kind of approach we should take to contemporary scores by women is exemplified in the title of a Desto recording of music by Miriam Gideon, Julia Smith, Louise Talma and Mabel Daniels that came out in 1972. The record was called simply "Four American Composers." The record producer saw no need to label these composers as women composers.

The commissions that the Fromm Foundation began giving women in the 1970s did not result from any change in policy. That is, we did not make a special attempt to seek out women composers. What happened instead was that there were more and more women composers of the younger generation who came to the attention of our commissioning committee, along with newly emerging male composers.

Our approach to contemporary women composers should also include making room not for just the top composers, but for women composers at all levels—as we do for men. Making room for composers at all levels is important because we need to give them space to explore and fail and be able to try again, to be part of the total fabric.

You might be asking yourselves at this point, does a great woman composer really need female forerunners? Can't she build on male traditions? To answer these questions, consider that women have achieved their greatest literary success, as Virginia Woolf points out in her feminist treatise, *A Room of One's Own*, not in epic poetry or drama, old forms that were hardened and set by men, but in the novel—a form that was still young and pliable at the time that women were beginning to write professionally. A form, therefore, that women could help shape.

Perhaps there is a parallel in music history. During what we like to call the common practice period—Bach to Brahms—music was being written in forms established by men. In our time musical form is again young and unshaped. Women composers thus have the opportunity to create musical syntax, generate form, to contribute to musical tradition right alongside men. And, not surprisingly, there are not only more women writing music, but more women writing music of strength and originality.

This does not, of course, mean that we will end up with two traditions of musical composition—one male and one female. That did not happen in novel-writing, and there is no reason to suppose that it would happen to music. In the novel tradition there is instead a richness that comes from the participation of both men and women, a richness that both men and women writers can draw upon and benefit from. Margaret Mead once made a comment that sheds some light on this subject. She wrote:

"Throughout history the more complex activities have been defined and redefined, now as male, now as female—sometimes as drawing equally on the gifts of both sexes. When an activity to which each sex could have contributed is limited to one sex, a rich, differentiated quality is lost from the activity itself."

As Margaret Mead's explanation makes clear, the point is not only that women artists need their own tradition, but that the arts themselves need both men and women practitioners to be fully expressive of human thought and feeling.

· · · · · · · · · · · · · · · · ·

Music Criticism in the
Pluralistic Eighties

This address was presented on August 12, 1985, to the Critics Conference in Aspen, Colorado, that took place in conjunction with the first "Fromm Week" of the Aspen Music Festival.

About the only excuse I can offer for what might otherwise seem presumptuous —a discussion of music criticism—is that it is just possible that I can trace my lineage back to the first music critic in recorded history, King Saul, who hurled his javelin at his harpist, David, when the music failed to soothe him. He missed his mark, *Gott sei Dank,* and David was able to go on to further triumphs.

Seriously, I am appearing before you, quite simply, because of my eagerness to promote and improve the cultural climate for music. My credentials consist of over sixty years spent listening to music and my continuing desire to increase my own capacities and awareness as a listener. Also, I have a profound longing to live in a community where the significance of music is recognized as an integral part of cultural and intellectual life, where the sustenance and development of the music of our own time is a deeply felt responsibility.

Since music criticism is the only available channel of general information on music, I have always turned to it with hopeful expectancy. And I would, therefore, hope that music criticism could achieve its highest potential.

I am aware that critics have a peculiarly thankless task. Professional evaluators— whether they are bank examiners or members of a hospital accreditation team or music critics—cannot both do their job properly and win popularity contests among the people they are evaluating. For many composers and performers, the only good critic is a critic who admires their work. Criticism of critics is always in season, it seems. A widely quoted statement by the late Mayor Daley may not be an exaggeration of people's response to the critics. Do you remember when he exclaimed, "They have vilified me, they have crucified me, yes, they have even criticized me." Rhetorically, Mayor Daley's statement is an example of anticlimax, but I am not at all sure that many composers and performers would consider the order—vilify, crucify, criticize—anticlimactic.

It is not my intention today either to rail against critics or to defend critics against their detractors. I said earlier that I would wish that music criticism could achieve its highest potential. I agree with the late Harold Rosenberg that "the major function of the critic is to improve the intellectual environment in which the creation of art takes place." While composers and performers influence the cultural climate by the nature and quality of their work, the professional music critic—because of the position he or she holds—has great influence on the way in which the work of composers and performers is understood. He has the power to help or hinder his readers in achieving enlightened and informed contact with the musical activity around them.

Musical activity today is peculiar. On the one hand, there is the staleness of the performance industry, which has long held our orchestras, opera companies, and major recitalists in thrall. On the other hand, there is the openness and rich diversity of the new music scene, which we have come to this conference to celebrate, and to which, increasingly, we head, as to an oasis.

It must be particularly exhilarating to be a music critic right now. You are encountering things for which you don't have labels, fresh sounds, unabashed musical expressivity, interesting musical ideas and interesting relationships between music and language and between music and other performing arts or media. And you are under no pressure to speculate about whether one style or compositional method will outlast the others.

This situation offers music critics an unparalleled opportunity to improve the intellectual environment of music and provide leadership to the rest of the music community. I would like to suggest that you take advantage of this opportunity by leading us in doing three things.

I

My first suggestion is that you work to maintain and improve the openness that characterizes the pluralism of the new music scene at its best by focusing on the uniqueness and on the quality of individual works and avoiding easy labeling or, even worse, setting up opposition between styles of composition or ignoring works that are not part of a "new trend."

What I have particularly missed in music criticism in the past is a concentration on what must ultimately be the critical issue and the only real news in music: the awareness of the characteristics of individual compositions. Instead, reviewers have tended to obstruct the reader's awareness of the musical object by espousing an ideological position toward music—advocating a particular style as the leading style or, more often, rejecting a particular style or even rejecting a particular work by a composer because it was in what was thought to be the same "exhausted" style he or she had used before. Ideology is not really useful to music criticism because it concerns itself with the way things have been done in general rather than the way in which a particular thing has been done.

In the not-too-distant past, when we all expected one of the twentieth-century styles or compositional methods to triumph over the others, such an espousal by a critic could be defended as an attempt to pick the winning horse—and then make sure that the horse stayed ahead of the field.

At that time composers were under such terrific pressure to evolve, to take music a step further, that they themselves spoke about their music in ideological terms and saw themselves joined in the Battle of Styles and Methods. Here is composer Shulamith Ran describing this dilemma at a symposium in the early '70s:

> . . . Countless composers are using every conceivable means to create something that sounds like no one else. And the result does indeed sound like

no one we can identify. Except that it sounds like all the other countless unidentifiables trying to sound like no one else we know. . . . Perhaps the most difficult dilemma confronting a composer today is that pressure to "evolve." . . . While in previous days an evolutionary phase was allowed to be in existence for at least three-quarters of a century, nowadays . . . a phase seems to reach its zenith in but a few short years. This leads to an artificial manufacturing of a so-called "progress," a phenomenon probably with no precedent in the past.

If we now view musical pluralism as a permanent condition rather than as a period of transition and crisis, then it is inappropriate to think in terms of winners and losers. In the context of musical pluralism, ideology in music criticism is at its best an excuse for making judgments on the basis of the gross characteristics of pieces rather than on their special individual characteristics—for labeling music rather than describing it. At a lower level, it can be a way of castigating people whom the writer dislikes or disapproves of. Or it can be a way of helping or hurting whole groups of people economically. This sometimes happens innocently enough, when composers are typecast in the media and then condemned if they do not follow what is expected of the type.

No doubt ideology and its accompanying air of controversy make good copy. Conflicts between things and persons are quicker to arouse interest than serious information about what lies within those things or people. I am aware that the "our-side — their-side" formula, intellectually impoverished though it may be, seems to satisfy more the needs of a considerably larger number of public-communication purposes than capturing the aesthetic experience of an encounter with a work of art. I urge you not to give in to journalism's natural appetite for controversy.

In the presence of many diverse musical works, we do, of course, need to make some order out of the diffuseness. The need to generalize—to create categories—is understandable. And we look to music critics to help us order and make sense of the musical activity in our midst. Someone has said that the profession of critic came into being "partly because people wanted help in dealing with the proliferation of uniqueness." In doing this *necessary* generalizing, I urge critics to be on their guard against three temptations:

1) the temptation to allow a generalization about a work to take the place of a description of the unique characteristics of the work;

2) the temptation to see different musical styles as being in opposition to one another; and

3) the temptation to value a work highly because a large number of composers are writing in a similar style. Or, what may be worse, to undervalue a work because it does not fit in with what appears to be the trend of the moment. What relevance is there in the question of how many composers are doing a particular kind of thing at a particular time? There is, after all, only one *Tristan and Isolde*, only one *Theory of Relativity*, only one *Finnegan's Wake*, only one *Principia Mathematica*. What if no one was ever inspired to imitate or develop a given musician's ideas? Does this mean that his work should not have existed, or that it had no value as a creation of the human imagination? A journalistic world where uniqueness is negatively associated with value and quality is indeed at odds with our intellectual and cultural traditions. How many

fugue composers would there have to be to justify the works of J. S. Bach?

You may well ask at this point, "Are you trying to tell us that being music critics in the midst of a musical pluralism means that we should not evaluate musical works, but merely describe them?"

My answer is No—although if I thought you and all the other critics would answer in the affirmative, I would be perversely tempted to answer Yes. It would be interesting to see what kind of reviews would be written if music critics deliberately limited themselves to describing what they heard. I suspect that evaluation would color the description in subtle ways; and the result might be first-rate criticism.

I must answer the question honestly, however, because there is a danger that the acknowledgment of *musical pluralism* can become a belief in *critical relativism*—a belief that no one musical work is any more valuable than another. However, accepting the idea that works in many styles can be equally good and that style itself is not a criterion of quality does not mean that we have to accept the idea that all musical works are equally good. It is always necessary to sort out the significant from the trivial. Uniqueness is not necessarily excellence.

There are many different works in many different styles. In one sense they are equal. But no one person can prefer them all. It is important to distinguish sharply between a work's right to exist and one's own preference for one work over another.

To make this distinction a music critic must be very clear about his own musical biases, admitting them not only privately, but also keeping readers constantly informed of them. I would like to say in passing here that I am not raising the issue of subjective music criticism versus objective music criticism because I assume that by now everyone accepts the idea that objective criticism is an impossibility. We do not value the music criticism of George Bernard Shaw any less because he could make statements like the following:

> Certain things one can say without hesitation. For example, that Elgar could turn out Debussy and Stravinsky music by the thousand bars for fun in his spare time.

As Joseph Kerman made clear in an article in the *Critical Inquiry* a few years ago, even academic music analysis is subjective in that it takes the masterpiece status of the work for granted.

The important thing is not to try to avoid being subjective—it is unavoidable—but to keep from encouraging or even allowing readers to interpret your subjective judgments as objective standards. In other words, admit your subjectivity, but don't try to pass it off as objectivity. Don't objectify your biases. Let us ask ourselves which pair of statements is typical of our attitude toward a musical work:

I like it; therefore it is of value.
I don't like it; therefore it is of no value.

or

I can see that it is of value, but I don't happen to like it.
It is probably trash, but I happen to love trash.

Music critics might even find it useful to publish a profile of their own musical taste—and refer to it later on in reviews both as a reminder to themselves and as a caution to readers.

It is probably not necessary to go as far in distinguishing preferences from judgments, as the English art critic Quentin Bell suggests when he writes, also in *Critical Inquiry,* "To appreciate that which is difficult to like makes one a member of the elite." But as the eighteenth-century music critic, Dr. Burney, wrote, "A good critic must have an enlarged taste, admiring whatever is good in its kind. . . ." And it is certainly important for critics to avoid using their own likes and dislikes, their own biases, to legislate what other people ought to be interested in, or more especially, what they ought not to be interested in.

II

Now the critic may ask, "How is it possible to criticize—that is describe and evaluate—new works? Can I really be expected to evaluate or even communicate the sense of a piece I have heard only once to readers who have never heard it and have never studied music?" One of the most valuable services a critic can render is to point out explicitly that a single hearing of something as complex as even the simplest musical composition is hardly a satisfactory way to experience it. If being uninformed qualifies one to make a judgment, nothing that is sophisticated or complex will be valued. Yet Western culture places it highest value on achieving coherence where there are many levels of meaning. If a work were judged solely on the basis of a single encounter, what would one think of the creations of Faulkner, Joyce, or Jackson Pollock? What judging on a single hearing tends to encourage in part is the promulgation of facile, readily evocative music. It takes a secure and self-critical critic to admit that he is unable to publish a valid judgment from one hearing of a difficult new work.

However, first impressions expressed immediately have their own validity. That is what makes journalistic music criticism peculiarly valuable. After all, interesting first encounters are what send one back to a work for a second experience of it. Ned Rorem has said that it is easier to recognize the real thing when you hear it than to recognize the absence of the real thing. Also, first encounters are unique. Different works affect one at different times because of what one brings to listening to a work or because of the way it is performed. Think back to the times when you found yourself overwhelmed by a musical work. On how many of these occasions were you hearing the piece for the first time? I remember my first encounter with Stravinsky's *Rite of Spring* in 1928 in Frankfurt, Germany. I can't say that I understood it, but, musically speaking, it made a twentieth-century man out of me and left me determined to take some active part in the musical life of this century. I have heard *Rite of Spring* many times since then and understand it better and am far more able to appreciate it as one of the important landmark works of our century. Yet I cherish the memory of that first hearing. *It is in connection with attentive listening that I wish to make my second suggestion to music critics, which is that you take advantage of the freshness of the new music to lead us in renewing and intensifying the way we listen to music.*

I wish there were some way to test the brain waves of people in the audience during a concert, to test exactly what is going in through our ears to the brain. Probably there is a way to do this, but no one has thought to put it to the test that I would like to have done. I fully expect that most of us audience members would discover that we are actually listening only a small portion of the time. Our listening is likely to become more alert if something is irregular about the performance, if the performance is not quite what we expected. I think we listen harder to extremely bad performances than we do to routinely good ones. We may even listen more alertly to bad performances than we do to great ones, especially if they are great performances of music we have heard over and over again. The fact that we are not listening may be partly why we often get so bored at concerts.

This habit of not listening to familiar music has even influenced the way we have listened to unfamiliar scores. At some point during the '60s we all discovered that a great many new scores sounded very much alike. We may have regretted that this was true, but at the same time, it meant that when we went to concerts where new scores were played, we didn't have to work so hard as we might have expected to before we made this discovery. Some of us made the discovery earlier than others. Others were still trying to hear little differences so that they could write about them or discuss them after the concert. We realized that what we should pay attention to was what the composer wrote in the program notes. Not only did some totally organized music sound alike, but indeterminate music sounded much like totally organized music. And depending upon whether we were more attracted by the idea of control or happenstance, we talked ourselves into preferring one method to the other. We even got to the point where the more difficult the music was to listen to, the better we thought it was. We began to equate merit with incomprehensibility.

I have welcomed the musical pluralism of the '80s because I believe that, if we let it, it can help us to listen to music again. I am asking nothing less than that we put ourselves in training for listening to music; that we prepare for listening by being at the peak of our physical alertness, not dulled with food and drink; that we evaluate our listening habits critically—find out how long we can listen intently and gradually attempt to increase our attention span; that we do exercises in aural perception.

Revitalizing the way we listen to music can go far to bring us closer not just to the new music, but to all music, and to help music regain its value.

III

Music itself has been the chief casualty of the emphasis on stardom in our concert life. The problem is that in the performance industry the stakes are high. There is much fame to be earned and much money to be made, and there is tremendous competition for both. Performers no longer pit themselves against a musical task or a musical problem demanding solution. Instead, they pit themselves against other performers. Because of this, the musical works themselves must be familiar. Viewed this way, musical works are like the school figures used in ice-skating competitions. They are played less because they are interesting in themselves than because they provide a way to rank the performers. This is a harsh comparison. But as our performers keep playing the same fifty pieces—as Virgil Thomson called them—over and over again, it is hard not to feel that they are just tracing figure 8's into the ice. The significance of a concert seems to be whether so-and-so's figure 8 wasn't just a little more graceful or more sweeping or bolder than so-and-so's. The relationship between music and its performance has become a vicious circle. Because the same works are played over and over, the focus is on performance rather than on the music. But also, because of the focus on performance, the same works are played over and over. Audiences conditioned to want only these fifty works are in danger of confusing musical culture with a kind of musical "Olympics." That reduces the task of the music critic to the dulling routine of comparing the performances of the same standard works over and over again. May I just add that for the music lover, almost every performance of a Beethoven symphony is great because the work is great.

It is my hope that the new music with its freshness and diversity may be able to revitalize our musical life. However, I have a deep fear that what we call the pluralism of the new music scene may not be hardy enough to keep flourishing surrounded by the big business of the performance industry. For one thing, the tendency of performance as entertainment or as business is to neutralize music, to erode the uniqueness of musical works, to smooth out the differences between them. When a technically brilliant performance is valued more than a stylistically penetrating one, Haydn begins to sound like Beethoven.

My third request of music critics is that you lead us in taking advantage of the qualities of the new music to renew our efforts to get our orchestras to play some of these scores. Here I call on you to use your journalistic skills in addition to your critical faculties, to be informed watchdogs, to remind our musical custodians of their responsibilities to music.

It may be our last chance in this century to readjust the balance between performance and music by revitalizing our stale orchestra repertory. The results of the poll the San Francisco Symphony management recently took of their subscribers indicate that symphony subscribers may be more receptive to new music than most symphony managers think they are. Forty-eight percent of the San Francisco subscribers who were asked how they felt about new music on the subscription series said they enjoyed it. Forty-eight percent. Another thirty percent responded that, while they may not like new music, they felt it is still important to hear.

I would like to suggest three ways that music critics can help to revitalize the performance industry.

1) The first is to encourage music directors and other conductors to repeat the new works with which they have had some success. I was disappointed a few years ago when Zubin Mehta did not take advantage of the success he had in the U.S. premiere of Boulez's *Notations* and repeat the score the following seasons.

Conductors should be encouraged to think of the first performances of any work new to an orchestra as auditions for that orchestra's permanent repertory. One test is not enough and would not be enough even if our audiences had filled in the fifty-year gap in their experience of twentieth-century music. The idea is, as Heinz Van-Royen, Artistic Director of the Concertgebouw, has expressed it, "to have a limited number of contemporary works in the repertoire and to repeat them from time to time. Music is better served if we make a careful selection and concentrate more on quality and on regular performances."

2) A second way music critics can help revitalize the performance industry is to use the power of the press to urge both government and private funding agencies to

expand their concept of the *challenge grant*. I have never understood why funding agencies challenge orchestras and opera houses merely to raise money. Why not give them money only on the condition that they increase the twentieth-century content of their repertory. The problem with challenge grants without any artistic conditions attached is that they reward performing groups for becoming good fund raisers.

3) A third way critics can help revitalize the performance industry is by suggesting that peformance organizations adopt a new concept for the term *audience development*, that they move from thinking of audience development as a euphemism for corralling ticket buyers to thinking of audience development as a deliberate plan for helping audiences go through a process of growth, differentiation, and evolution vis-à-vis music.

My hope of living in a community where the significance of music is recognized as an integral part of cultural and intellectual life, where the sustenance and development of the music of our own time is a deeply felt responsibility, is not likely to be realized in my lifetime or yours or in anyone's. But if we can work together to preserve and enhance the spirit of openness in our music life, if we can let the fresh vitality of the new music inspire us to listen more intently to music, and if we continue our efforts to revitalize the repertory of our large performing organizations, we may increase the small but growing band of listeners who believe that no art can be more important to them than the art that is created in their midst, however rich the legacy of the past may be.

A Contemporary Role
for American Music Libraries

Originally presented at a meeting of the Music Library Association on January 21, 1966 in Chicago, this address was subsequently printed in the Spring-Summer 1966 issue of Perspectives of New Music *(v. 4, no. 2, pp. 140-143).*

The American music of our time, as by now should be unmistakably clear to all of us, belongs to the development of American thought, not to the development of our entertainment or to the gratification of more or less deep-seated socio-psychological drives. Whether this has always been true about music is, no doubt, debatable. But that our own music has persistently had this function, whether we approved of it or liked it or not, is indisputable. The fact is that the intellectual vitality of our music has created, now at last, a really strong and unmistakable national character for American composition. And this is the case whether or not we, or even our composers, necessarily believe that this is a healthy condition for musical development. In this way, American music has been like every contemporary field, where the coming to terms with the intellectual necessities of the twentieth century has liberated limitless new possibilities. And the natural result of this is an internal vigor and excitement in the compositional profession itself; not only are gifted people increasingly attracted to it, but their enthusiasm and energy is creating a wholly new and full musical life within the university, a life in which the composer himself, at least, can fully realize his musical ideas and aspirations.

But just because it is a field whose vigorous contemporary aspect is its unbounded intellectual adventurousness, our new music is being led, by the very strength of this new direction, further and further from our culture's awareness. Composers, after all, whatever their feelings as social human beings, reach professional and artistic fulfillment in composing their music and hearing it played. They have now even ceased to impinge on the general consciousness by their professional distress, for they have found that they can satisfactorily generate conditions under which this fulfillment can be reached on their own, without waiting any longer for society's benevolence.

In the past, they at least reached society's awareness by appealing to its social conscience, an area much more sensitive than its musical or cultural conscience. But now that we cannot even jog our consciences by asserting that it is our duty to support our composers whether we like their work or not, we are forced to confront the much more disquieting necessity of deciding whether or not we need composers.

The choice is clear: either we provide an intermediary link through which the composer's work continues to be made publicly available for society's benefit, or we permit music to slip from our grasp, to develop out of our hearing and observation to the point where we of the intellectually aware and interested public are excluded from sharing in its discoveries and revelling in its imaginative insights. For those of us for whom, from our very earliest intellectual lives, music has occupied as fundamental a place as reading and thinking of any kind, the loss would be catastrophic, unthinkable. But it would not be the composers whom we could blame for this situation, however much it may arise from qualities in their work—any more than we would blame Carnap, Wittgenstein, Einstein, Planck, or Yang and Lee for their independent thoughts and for their discoveries which are difficult for us to understand. Every creative thinker—and everything in our Western intellectual tradition affirms this view—has not only the right but indeed the obligation to follow his discoveries to their ultimate implications; we would have to impugn his intellectual and creative integrity if he did otherwise. Thus we as a culture have given him his mandate, and we must be grateful that he has taken it up so unequivocally and with such unflinching courage.

An intermediary link does exist, however, between creative intellection and the cultural public. That link is, it seems to me, virtually the definition of one of our most important cultural institutions—the one whose distinguished representatives I am addressing today. The historic role of the library in supporting scholarship by making its essential tools available to the scholar, and, in exchange, making the discoveries of the scholar accessible to the public, is fundamental. This role can, like the contemporary fields of knowledge themselves, undergo a twentieth-century revaluation that could yield spectacular results in extending our cultural horizons to the limits of contemporary thought. For just as university libraries take it as their responsibility to make available to any interested person the latest developments in any field of knowledge, so music libraries can undertake to offer to their communities an awareness of the contemporary state of music. This, of course, can be done only through the dissemination of new musical works—the true end-products of musical thinking—in the one form in which they can be made available for study and performance: scores. And, on the other hand, just as university presses and university libraries make it their particular responsibility to preserve and disseminate the work done in their own scholarly communities, so music libraries, it seems to me, have a special responsibility for preserving and disseminating the work of the composers in their own communities.

Now, since every music librarian is already faced with the problem of selection from all published scores of new music, you may wonder what special new revaluation of the music libraries' function I have in mind. Precisely this: the anomalous cultural position that left new music for so long at the mercy of the entertainment and commercial worlds also left its publication in the hands of commercial presses. But, in all fairness, let me state that, even with the best intentions, it would be economically prohibitive for our American music publishers to make all important American musical developments publicly available. So, since long before the Second World War, and certainly ever since its end, much extremely significant compositional work has either remained totally unpublished and unavailable, or has at best had its publication delayed for an intolerably long period of time. But our publishers themselves can hardly bear the full blame for this: the list of insurmountable obstacles to commercial publication of new music in this country is too long and—especially to an audience like this—too familiar to warrant detailed exposition here. It should, however, be pointed out that the apparent superiority of European publishers in this area does not truly reflect on our own publishing conditions. European publishers not only have the standard-repertory works in their catalogs that provide a basic financial endowment for their whole operation, but the new music they publish is given widespread radio, television, orchestra, and—especially—opera house performances that actually make the activity economically realistic. Again, I need hardly spell out the nature of the corresponding American situation.

In America, it has become common practice among composers themselves to compensate for this lack of publication by exchanging reproductions of their own manuscript scores. In this sense, then, scores do exist and could be made available if a proper medium and procedure existed for doing so within the music-library structure. If there were some way for all our music libraries to gain access to the most important of these unpublished scores, to be able to buy them, publicize their existence and nature, and make them available in further reproduction, then the possibility of realizing the library's true function in preserving musical culture would become much more real. And, further, if the library's interest thus manifested were to encourage university presses to publish new musical works as they do other original, creative, intellectual work, the absurdity of our new music having to compete for survival in the commercial publication world with Broadway shows, piano-teaching pieces, and football band classics would at last be an end.

Obviously, the problem lies in the machinery through which such scores could be located, chosen, listed, and disseminated. And, of course, there is the related question of how all this could be financed within the narrow limits of normal library resources. But I believe that only a small, imaginative extension of the traditional library function as a servant of its regional intellectual community would set the machinery in motion. And I believe that the active interest of such culturally prestigious institutions as our nation's major music libraries would in itself provide the pressure necessary to release this much needed economic support from the appropriate sources.

To begin with, the great advantage possessed by each music library is its awareness of its own community, of the composers therein, and of the direction of the most vigorous and important work. In this country there are about 250 music libraries of major importance. I would propose that each music library adopt the most important composers living in its area in order to build up a catalog of scores that would constitute a total representation of these composers' works. Then, I would recommend the establishment of an independent agency, administered by and attached to one of the leading music libraries, that would serve as a clearing house for contemporary music by publishing an annual catalog listing the contents of each library's "adopted composer" collection of scores. Such a center could also function as a channel through which requests for copies of scores could be transmitted and expedited. It could also dispense grants to member libraries to make it possible for them to send reproductions of scores to any legitimate applicants, whether other libraries, university music departments, or performing groups. Given the enormous value accruing to such an activity in relation to the modesty of even its maximum cost, one could assume that organizations that already divert extensive sums into the dissemination of music— such as BMI, ASCAP, and the major foundations—could be appealed to for the necessary economic support. Such organizations would no longer be in the position of having to buy new music as a commodity in a nonexistent commercial market, but would actually be providing support not only for compositional activity as a whole but for performance, and not only locally, but—at least—in every American university community.

Details of this nature obviously present no significant obstacle. What does lie in our path, however, is the need for the fundamental conviction that would inspire such a massive involvement in the musical present. But any uneasiness, any qualms about our new music's "ultimate place in history" can hardly be sustained. The only history in which we can presume to judge or even be legitimately concerned with contemporary music is our own. To what other history could our music belong? And if, in preserving the record of the musical history of our time, our music libraries succeed in preserving our musical culture itself, what more significant historic role could they ever hope to fulfill?

The Role of Symphony Boards

This address was given for the trustees and overseers of The Boston Symphony Orchestra on April 23, 1981. It was subsequently printed in the October/November 1981 issue (pp. 22-25) of Symphony Magazine, the official publication of the American Symphony Orchestra League.

I n 30 years of serving on boards I've been through a long period of consciousness-raising—if I may call it that—and I've come to the conclusion that lay board members can play a far more significant role in any organization than they usually do. They should not, of course, ever trespass upon the territory of the professional. Rather, the kind of role they play must evolve from their own increasing understanding of the needs and goals of the organization and of the public it serves.

I have seen too many boards whose tasks were restricted to fund-raising—where the board members were assumed to have all the money and the professionals all the brains, where the board members were looked down on by the professionals as stuffed shirts and the professionals looked on by the board members as being one rung down on the social ladder. I'm sure that at least the *latter* kind of patronizing could not take place here in Boston. I recall an ad for the *Boston Globe* quoting Mark Twain: "In New York, they ask, 'How much is he worth?' In Philadelphia, 'Who were his parents?' In Boston, 'How much does he know?'" But all joking aside, I *have* attended board meetings—far too many—in which the participants merely approved minutes and listened to sugar-coated reports of achievements, too many board meetings that were simply pleasant social gatherings, meetings of a mutual admiration society in which the professionals flattered the laymen and the laymen fawned on the professionals.

It is true that in most voluntary organizations the layman's task begins with fund-raising. But it should not end there. At the very least, the board owes contributors the assurance that the funds are being spent judiciously. For that reason alone, board members must be able to judge whether or not their organization's operations serve its true purposes.

That lay board members are in a special position to make this kind of judgment seems clear. The professional staff spend their working hours looking at their jobs from the inside out; they are necessarily preoccupied with professional issues and values. But lay board members look at the organization from the outside in; as representatives of the organization's constituencies, they are able to view the organization in terms of its role in the community it serves, to see it from a social perspective, and can therefore be a force for constructive change.

But let's narrow our focus to the symphony orchestra. A symphony orchestra presents *music* to an *audience*—whether in live concerts, broadcasts, or recordings—and in doing so, its purpose is twofold: to serve music (in the words of Koussevitzky, "We must not use music; we must serve it") and to serve the audience. (In the last analysis, music exists for the audience.) These two purposes often seem to be in conflict, but essentially they are not. They are really two aspects of the same purpose. If a symphony orchestra devotes itself to serving music, it cannot fail to serve the best interests of its audience. The contrary is also true; when an orchestra no longer serves music, when, instead, it uses music, then it no longer serves the best interests of its audience.

Serving music does not merely mean *playing music well.* If it did, we would have few complaints. Our 20th-century orchestras have achieved a level of performance unknown in previous eras—possibly because they've been rehearsing the same works for 50 years. I am reminded of a conversation that reportedly took place at Glyndebourne. An American visitor, impressed by the quality of the Glyndebourne lawn, asked his English host, "How do you suppose they got the lawn so thick and velvety?" The native replied, "They've been mowing it for four hundred years."

No, serving music means playing it *in order that it might be heard.* For that reason the most important service a symphony orchestra can perform for both music itself and its audience lies in its programming. Programming is unfortunately also the most neglected area of orchestra policy.

We've been experiencing the result of this neglect for some time now. For one thing, the existing orchestra repertory has been shrinking at an alarming rate.

For another thing, we now have a 50-year gap in the permanent repertory of our orchestras. Recently I had occasion to ask a sophisticated music lover to name the works composed within the last 50 years which he felt he could recognize, not by name, but by ear. He could name only three works: Bartok's *Concerto for Orchestra,* Stravinsky's *Symphony of Psalms,* and Hindemith's *Suite from Mathis der Mahler.* Two of these, by the way, were Boston Symphony commissions.

Thirdly, the programming of the music that does get played is incoherent. Works that are played together are not required to make sense together. A whole season's programming is just a series of more or less brilliant "attractions"; it does not possess any kind of *Gestalt.* But, as symphony-goers, we do not need to be told these things. We're already experiencing them. Let's take a moment to explore some of our mutual symphony-going experiences:

Most of us would like an orchestra concert to be something special, to be, as Margaret Mead said, "a celebration, of which our lives have so few." We want to be taken out of the routineness of our daily lives. But we find that orchestra concerts themselves seem routine, predictable. They regularly begin with an innocuous curtain-raiser, followed by a flashy concerto played by a flashy soloist, and end with a big piece chosen from the Romantic or post-Romantic periods. We sometimes show up at concerts without even bothering to remind ourselves what's on the program. The concerts are more like tranquilizers than stimulants. And we wonder, have we lost our taste for orchestral music somewhere along the way? Or is it just that we keep hearing the same pieces again and again?

Few of us have any real sense of being part of a community of music listeners. How often do we feel compelled to gather over a cup of coffee and eagerly, even heatedly, discuss the music we've just heard?

Even when the orchestra interrupts its routine programming to play a new work, most of us are not so much excited by it as bewildered. We have no frame of reference in which to place the new work; nothing that we've heard—either on the same program or on earlier programs—illuminates the work for us. The work is unpredictable, and in the context we're hearing it, it's more bewildering than stimulating. We know we'll never hear it again anyway, so we just forget about it.

Since the human mind is always seeking connnections, we often try to figure out just what's behind concert programming. Why did the conductor choose to perform these particular works on the same program? Is there some connection that we are meant to perceive? Apparently not. When a new season is announced we also look in vain for links between programs. At best, we sometimes find that one composer is featured in several programs (often because of an ongoing recording project).

Many of us have attended symphony concerts for years and yet we have the uneasy feeling that we don't really have a grasp of orchestral music as a whole. There seem to be gaps in our experience, not only in our experience of 20th-century music, but also in our experience of music of the distant past.

Why has orchestra programming been so neglected? It has long been the practice of orchestra boards to select a music director and then leave the concert programming to his discretion—which has often meant leaving it only to his personal tastes (which is the way it ought to be), but also to the demands of his recording contracts or touring plans, or even to the relative bargaining power of his guest conductors and soloists. All of this pushing and pulling can hardly be expected to result in coherent programming. It's a miracle that our orchestra programs are even as interesting as they are.

The time is overdue for orchestra boards, as representatives of the audience, to work closely with music directors, administrators, representative orchestra members, and other professional musicians within their communities to formulate a permanent philosophy of programming for their orchestras. Such a philosophy would provide the orchestra with a continuing musical identity, an identity sorely needed in this time when music directors are not truly *resident* music directors and guest conductors come and go, bringing their specialties with them and taking them away again.

As a working model we might consider the structure of orchestra programming suggested by William Schuman at last year's meeting of the American Symphony Orchestra League. He envisioned three parts:

1.) the systematic and continuing exploration of the great literature of the past on a rotating basis over a period of years;

2.) the systematic and purposeful effort to develop a repertory of contemporary works that have already found favor; and

3.) the introduction of new works, by both established composers and newer ones.

Parts *Two* and *Three* of Schuman's proposals are the most difficult to put into practice. The best solution would be to have music directors who are committed to keeping the orchestra repertory alive and growing, and who don't just perform contemporary scores but fight for them as Koussevitzky used to. If Koussevitzky played a new work one season and the audience was less than enthusiastic, that didn't scare him. He'd give it right back to them the next season. The *Seventh Symphony* of Sibelius, written in 1924, was played by the BSO in 1926, 1931, 1933, 1935, 1937, 1939, 1941, and 1946. The point is that because he believed in a work, Koussevitzky also believed that it was important that the audience get to know the work.

Music directors who have no inclination to fight for works that are unpopular can at least make a point of repeating their successes. Zubin Mehta, for example, should take advantage of the success he had in the U.S. premiere of Boulez's *Notations* last winter and repeat the score next season. So, too, the Metropolitan Opera should capitalize on their current success, *Parade*—the trio of one-acters by Satie, Poulenc, and Ravel. But reports indicate that neither *Notations* nor *Parade* are scheduled for future performances. We applaud Seiji Ozawa for his commitment to the *Second Symphony* of Peter Maxwell Davies. Mr. Ozawa not only premiered this 55-minute work in Boston, but also performed it in New York and on the recent transcontinental tour of the BSO, thus defying the warnings of the organizers of concerts that the presentation of such long and complex new works would be box office poison. As so often, the experts were wrong. Wherever the BSO played the symphony they were greeted by a full and enthusiastic house. We hope Mr. Ozawa will later bring the symphony back to Boston in order to integrate it into the permanent repertory of the BSO.

We need to condition ourselves to think of the first performances of any work new to an orchestra as auditions for that orchestra's permanent repertory. One test is not enough and would not be enough even if our audiences had filled in the 50-year gap in their experience of 20th-century music. The idea is to have a limited number of contemporary works in the repertoire and to repeat them from time to time. Music is better served if we make a careful selection and concentrate more on quality and regular performances.

Orchestra boards with music directors who are not comfortable conducting contemporary music can follow the example of Cleveland, where contrast for the conservative programs of George Szell was provided by hiring Pierre Boulez as the principal guest conductor.

Another idea—and a practical one now that fees of star performers are fast becoming prohibitive for symphony orchestras, particularly in view of decreased federal funding—is to search out talented young conductors and soloists who would be thrilled to have an engagement with a major orchestra and would be willing to learn 20th-century scores or less familiar works from the past. If the performance of 20th-century music is assigned to a guest conductor who would not have to learn the music during orchestra rehearsals, no or very little additional rehearsal time would be needed.

To take advantage of the retrospective mood of the moment, an orchestra board and a music director might plan their own retreat into the past—not the distant past but the music of the last 50 years. They could appoint a group of musical advisers—not unlike the *dramaturgs* in German opera houses—who would draw up a list of works that had not been played at all or with any frequency. Some of these works could be assigned to guest conductors in rotation. After a few seasons the works could begin to be repeated until they became recognizable repertoire.

Establishing a permanent philosophy of programming for an orchestra will take both vision and ingenuity, I have no doubt, but if we can help our orchestra find a point of view and become a force for contemporary cultural advancement, it will be worth the effort.

To sum up the challenge facing us, I'd like to invoke Bernard Shaw. A character in *Heartbreak House* points out that the soul is a very expensive thing to keep. "It eats music and pictures and books and mountains and lakes and beautiful things. . . ." And she adds, "You can't have them without lots of money." And I would like to add, "Such things are not only expensive but highly fragile. You can't keep them without the dedication of men and women like yourselves."

THE FROMM
MUSIC
FOUNDATION

The Fromm Music Foundation: Past, Present, and Future

The following statement by Paul Fromm is excerpted from the booklet compiled in 1972 on the occasion of the twentieth anniversary of the Fromm Foundation, which also marked the Foundation's relocation to Harvard University.

On the twentieth anniversary of the Fromm Music Foundation it seems appropriate to place its aims, and the ways in which they have been realized, in some historical perspective. Our primary objective over these years has been to bridge the gap that exists between contemporary composers and society. From the very beginning we have endeavored to avoid the kind of highly structured organization that large institutional foundations, by virtue of their size and diverse activities, have been forced to adopt. Rather than entrusting policies and programs to an administrative staff, committees or trustees, we have actively involved as advisors in our work some of the most eminent members of the musical community. Their concerns, opinions, and suggestions have guided us in all our efforts. Our insistence on maintaining organizational flexibility has enabled us to reach out to composers, and to act in a variety of ways on behalf of individual artists without encroaching on their artistic independence.

The central purpose of the Fromm Music Foundation has been to restore to the composer his rightful position at the center of musical life. Rather than subsidizing institutions or supporting other, even more anonymous aspects of culture, the Fromm Foundation has chosen to focus its programs on individual artists, individual works, and individual musical situations.

Our programs have been deliberately designed to avoid the kind of patronage that traditionally has provided broad support for a particular musical activity or a particular group of artists. Instead, we have tried to create a continuing series of model activities which, by their example, will act as stimulants to musical creativity and contribute to the development of a healthy musical environment.

Our commitment to music as a living art has taken us in several directions, all focused on bringing about meaningful interactions among composers, performers and audiences. Specifically, we have sought to influence the contemporary musical scene by:

- Commissioning young and relatively unknown composers, as well as established composers
- Providing the best possible conditions for the performance of contemporary music

- Sponsoring (jointly with the Berkshire Music Center) the annual Tanglewood Festival of Contemporary Music, as part of a comprehensive program for the study and performance of contemporary music
- Subsidizing recordings and sponsoring special radio programs
- Sponsoring seminars for composers and critics, and supporting the magazine *Perspectives of New Music*

Our program of commissioning, along with its related activities, has been guided by these simple truths: all music is modern music in its own time, and music as an art will cease to exist if a living flow of musical creation no longer reaches a concerned and interested public. Merely stating these truths serves to bring into focus the anomalous status of the composer in contemporary society. Although his creativity is the source of musical culture, the increasing imbalance between artistic and commercial values has generally denied him a recognition commensurate with the importance of his function, while simultaneously denying our society contact with music that expresses its own sensibilities.

The Fromm Music Foundation's program of commissioning and other supportive efforts are attempts to reverse the mood of public apathy described by Aaron Copland in his book *Music and Imagination*:

> The worst feature of the composer's life is the fact that he does not feel himself an integral part of the musical community. There is no deep need for his activities as composer, no passionate concern in each separate work as it is written. When a composer is played, he is usually surrounded by an air of mild approval. When he is not played, no one demands to hear him.

Our aim in awarding commissions has been to stimulate the initiative of composers so that they can contribute more fully to the development of a living musical culture. More specifically, we have sought to encourage composers whose works reveal pronounced musical conviction and individuality as well as professional craftsmanship.

When we commission new works, we also commit ourselves to channel these works into the mainstream of musical life. Our responsibilities to the composers have extended to the preparation of scores and parts, the arrangement of performances in such principal music centers as Tanglewood, New York, Boston, Chicago, Los Angeles, and San Francisco, and frequently to publication and recording.

That the Fromm Foundation now marks its twentieth anniversary is in itself of little importance. If, however, as I believe, our efforts on behalf of contemporary music were vital, our concern must now be to ensure that they remain vital. Human institutions stand ever in need of renewal and revitalization, and the time has come to end the era in which the Fromm Music Foundation was simply an extension of myself. We must move on to a new era, in which the Foundation must be able to exist independently of any one individual.

In order to assure a permanent role for the Foundation as a vital force in contemporary music, we are transferring its base of operations to Harvard University. The University's institutional stability and vast ever-renewing human resources will add new strength to the organization and functional structure of the Foundation. On September 1, 1972, the Foundation will become The Fromm Music Foundation at Harvard University.

In advancing the Foundation's purposes, we will continue programs that have proved effective in the past, and we will initiate new ones that, we hope, will further contribute to the development of a healthy composer-performer-audience relationship. While our activities will remain flexible and adaptable to the changing art scene, our basic policy must stand firm. This policy is best expressed in the words of John Maynard Keynes, who, on the creation of the British Arts Council, said, "The task of an official body in the arts is not to teach or censor but to give courage, confidence and opportunity to artists."

An Interview with Paul Fromm

The following interview with Paul Fromm was given to Raymond Morin of the Worcester Tele-
gram *and the* Evening Gazette *of Worcester, Massachusetts, in 1968. The following is not reprinted
from either newspaper but edited anew from a transcription of the original unabridged interview.*

R.M. Please tell me something of your early background leading to your interest in
music: family, musical training, and so on.

P.F. I was born in 1906 in Kitzingen, a small Bavarian town in Germany where my
father was a wine merchant. My formal education was not much to brag about.
At the age of fifteen I left school and began to earn my living by working for
a firm in Frankfurt am Main. There I came in contact with a great variety of
music, including contemporary music. Then, as today, the general public rejected
modern music and occasionally protested vociferously against it. In those days,
Bartok, Hindemith, Krenek, Milhaud, Schoenberg, and Stravinsky were the young
avant-garde composers. I was as fascinated by their music at that time as I am
today by the music of such contemporary composers as Babbitt, Carter, Copland,
Druckman, Foss, Kirchner, Schuller, Sessions, Shapey, and all the others.

I should mention my early encounter with Krenek's music in Germany. Krenek became my fellow immigrant and friend in the United States, and since the
establishment of the Fromm Foundation in 1952, he has received three commissions from us: for the opera *The Bell Tower, Sestina* for instrumental ensemble,
and *Quaestio Temporis*, an orchestral work. I always refused to believe that—at a
time when painters, writers, and poets cogently expressed themselves in the idiom
of their own time—our composers would wish to declare the status quo on an
art that through the centuries has never ceased to be in a continual state of
becoming.

As a child I was able to play the piano transcriptions of symphonies from
Beethoven to Bruckner to Mahler four hands with my brother, Herbert, who
became a professional musician. Herbert, a composer of note, is the retired Musical Director of Temple Israel in Boston.

R.M. I have heard conflicting reports on your business ties, one of which was Christian Brothers wines.

P.F. I founded Geeting and Fromm, Inc., wine importers in Chicago, perhaps the
smallest of the big firms in the field and surely the biggest of the small ones.
My firm is one of the last surviving independent companies. If I hadn't maintained this independence I could not operate on the principle: earn in the busi-

ness, spend on the Foundation. My brother Alfred's firm in San Francisco, Fromm & Sichel, Inc., is the national distributor of Christian Brothers wines.

R.M. Who was the first composer to activate your interest in new idioms?

P.F. The turning point that, musically speaking, made a twentieth-century man of me, came in 1927 in Frankfurt, Germany. I heard Stravinsky's *Rite of Spring* for the first time. This music was as new to our time as Beethoven's *Eroica* to his. It struck me like lightning. Here was vital music that was far less characterized by academic purity than by range and depth of expression. I never imagined back in 1927 that in 1968 I would have warmly inscribed photos of Stravinsky in my home and my office in Chicago.

R.M. What were the origins of the Fromm Music Foundation?

P.F. Ever since I arrived in the United States as an immigrant in 1938, I interested myself in the music and musical life of my adopted country. Soon I became concerned about the anomalous position the American composer occupies in our society. His creativity is the source of musical culture, but his status in the musical world is uncertain. Because of the deepening rift between artistic and commercial values, he is excluded from influencing and inspiring the direction of public taste. For years I pondered these problems and finally, in 1952, I was able to do something about them.

R.M. Do you feel that the contemporary composer is generally neglected by the public and performing musicians?

P.F. Music is a domain in which very little can be known outside the practitioner's work. Nobody can relate to—and even less form a judgment about—something that is not known to him. Older music (even if the particular work is new to the listener) can be understood in the context of the style of its period. There is no frame of reference for the general public when it encounters contemporary music for the first time.

R.M. Does the same neglect of contemporary music apply to the European scene?

P.F. In the United States we have universities and colleges offering our composers an environment in which they can survive economically and to a lesser extent function artistically. In Europe, the composers are supported by the royalties received from numerous performances by government-subsidized radio stations that have their own orchestras and their own performers and performing groups. Still, the wide dissemination of contemporary music in Europe is not necessarily synonymous with popular acceptance. Judging from the programs of European music festivals, the European public is even more apathetic toward contemporary music than American audiences.

R.M. Are the majority of contemporary American works performed in Europe representative of American accomplishment?

P.F. Just the contrary. The Atlantic curtain is virtually soundproof in its Easterly channel. Europe still discriminates against America for not having produced Bach, Mozart, and Beethoven.

75

R.M. Are music critics just or antagonistic in their evaluation of contemporary music?

P.F. Many music critics are unaware of the terms, contexts, characteristics, and implications of the compositions and activities of composers. As in the days of Wagner's contemporary, Hanslick, they still limit themselves by their one-dimensional view of a multifarious activity. While composers rejoice in each other's disparity, critics focus on an assumed antagonism among composers: Brahms vs. Wagner in the days of Hanslick, Schoenberg vs. Stravinsky, or Babbitt vs. Cage in our time. Critics do not always understand the richness of ideas and the innumerable unique degrees between these imagined "polar" points.

R.M. What is your reaction when you hear a new work? Do you ever suspect that it is deliberately revolutionary?

P.F. My reaction is to try to find what new musical ideas, what new insights into the world of sound structure I can gain by listening as intently as possible.

R.M. Are we in a period of chaotic experimentation?

P.F. I think we're in a period of enduring experimentation as we have been in music since about 875 A.D. Musical sound arises from adequate projections of a musical idea. Thus, in serious music, there is no such thing as "new" or "old" sound, only the unique sound of a unique composition.

R.M. Who decides what will survive from among the idioms that are new now, whether electronic music, chance music, etc.? Is it the public, composers, performing musicians, writers?

P.F. Those who adopt them for the needs of their ideas and thus make them articulate: the composers, of course.

R.M. Is much of the new music a true and inevitable reflection of present chaotic world conditions?

P.F. It is a true and inevitable reflection of the present state of the development of musical thought.

Works Commissioned by the
Fromm Music Foundation, 1952–1987

*The following is a list of the works commissioned by the Fromm Music Foundation during Paul
Fromm's lifetime. It effectively demonstrates Fromm's emphasis on the central function of the composer and of the individual work in musical life, that is, on creative activity. The majority of
these works received first performances with support from the Foundation. Most were premiered
at Foundation-sponsored concerts at the Festival of Contemporary Music at the Berkshire Music
Center, Tanglewood, at the Aspen Music Festival, or at annual Fromm concerts at Harvard
University and The University of Chicago.*

John Adams	work in progress for two pianos	—
Stephen Albert	*Voices Within* Concertino Ensemble	1975
Carlos Roque Alsina	*Auftrag* Chamber Ensemble	1967
T.J. Anderson	*Transitions* Chamber Ensemble	1971
Theodore Antoniou	*Events II* Orchestra	1969
	Epigrams Soprano and Chamber Ensemble	1981
Walter Aschaffenburg	*Cello Sonata*	1954
Daniel Asia	*Rivalries* Chamber Orchestra	1986
Milton Babbitt	*Vision and Prayer* Soprano and Synthesized Accompaniment	1961
	Canonical Form Piano	1983
Arthur Berger	*Chamber Concerto*	1962

Luciano Berio	*Circles*	1960
	Voice, Harp, and Two Percussion Players	
	work in progress for Voice, Viola, and Digital Processor	—
Gordon Binkerd	*Symphony No. 2*	1957
Easley Blackwood	*String Quartet No. 1*	1957
	Trio	1968
	Violin, Cello, and Piano	
Susan Blaustein	*Cello Concerto*	1984
	Cello and Chamber Orchestra	
Martin Boykan	*Trio*	1975
	Violin, Cello, and Piano	
Todd Brief	*Slow Lament*	1984
	Soprano and Piano	
Earle Brown	*Windsor Jambs*	1980
	Mezzo-soprano and Chamber Ensemble	
Elliott Carter	*Double Concerto*	1961
	Harpsichord, Piano, and Two Chamber Orchestras	
Robert Ceely	*Beyond the Ghost Spectrum*	1969
	Dancers, Chamber Ensemble, and Electronic Tape	
Paul Chihara	*Symphony in Celebration*	1975
	Orchestra	
Edward Cohen	*Elegy*	1977
	Soprano, Flute, Oboe, Clarinet, Violin, Viola, and Cello	
Ornette Coleman	*In Honor of NASA & Interplanetary Soloist*	1986
	Oboe and String Quartet	
Randolph Coleman	*Concerto*	1964
	Piano and Chamber Orchestra	
Michael Colgrass	*As Quiet As*	1966
	Orchestra	
Marc Antonio Consoli	*Fantasia Celeste*	1983
	Soprano and Chamber Ensemble	
George Crumb	*Music for a Summer Afternoon*	1974
	Two Amplified Pianos and Percussion	

Ingolf Dahl	*Quartet*	1957
	Violin, Viola, Cello, and Piano	
Mario Davidovsky	*Synchronisms No. 2*	1964
	Flute, Clarinet, Violin, and Cello	
	Inflexions	1967
	Fourteen Players	
David Del Tredici	*I Hear An Army*	1964
	Soprano and String Quartet	
William Denny	*String Quartet No. 2*	1956
Mark DeVoto	*The Distinguished Thing*	1968
	Piano and Chamber Ensemble	
David Diamond	*Woodwind Quintet*	1958
Charles Dodge	*Folia*	1965
	Chamber Ensemble	
Deborah Drattell	*Alone*	1984
	Soprano and Chamber Ensemble	
James Drew	*West Indian Lights*	1974
	Orchestra	
Jacob Druckman	*String Quartet No. 3*	1981
Edwin Dugger	*Intermezzi*	1969
	Chamber Ensemble	
John Eaton	*Concert Piece*	1967
	Syn-Ket and Orchestra	
Alvin Epstein	*Sabrina Fair*	1956
	Tenor, Violin, Viola, Cello, and Piano	
Richard Felciano	*Lamentations for Jani Christou*	1970
	Chamber Ensemble and Electronic Sounds	
Irving Fine	*Fantasia*	1957
	Violin, Viola, and Cello	
David Finko	*Septet*	1982
	Chamber Ensemble	
Lukas Foss	*Echoi*	1962
	Clarinet, Cello, Piano, and Percussion	
Primous Fountain	*Grudges*	1972
	Orchestra	
Arnold Franchetti	*Three Ricercari*	1958
	Fifteen Instruments	

Philip Fried	*Meditations and Satires* Soprano and Chamber Ensemble	1985
Kenneth Gaburo	*Antiphony III* Sixteen Singers and Tape	1967
Gerardo Gandini	*Hescha Sombra* Chamber Ensemble	1967
Celso Garrido-Lecca	*Paracas* Chamber Work for Three Instrumental Groups	1972
Emmanuel Ghent	*Lustrum* Chamber Ensemble	1974
Alberto Ginastera	*Cantata Para America Magica* Soprano, Thirteen Percussion Players, Celesta, and Two Pianos	1960
John Harbison	*Elegiac Songs* Mezzo-soprano and Chamber Ensemble	1973
Bernard Heiden	*Serenade* Bassoon, Violin, Viola, and Cello	1956
John C. Heiss	*Inventions, Contours, and Colors* Chamber Ensemble	1973
Robert Helps	*Serenade in Three Movements* Violin, Piano, Horn, and String Quartet	1964
Joel Hoffman	*Chamber Symphony* Chamber Orchestra	1980
	Music for Trumpets and Strings Two Trumpets and String Quartet	1982
Richard Hoffman	*Orchestra Piece*	1961
Alan Hovhaness	*The Stars* Soprano, Chorus, English Horn, Celeste, Harp, and Strings	1955
	To The God Who Is In The Fire Men's Voices and Percussion	1957
Joseph Hudson	Composition	c.1975
John Huggler	*Sinfonia for Thirteen Players*	1974
Lee Hyla	*Pre-pulse Suspended* Chamber Orchestra	1984
Andrew Imbrie	*String Quartet No. 3*	1957

Ben Johnston	*Desolation* Written for The Swingle Singers	1980
Betsy Jolas	*Tales of a Summer Sea* Orchestra	1977
Carson Kievman	*Wake Up, It's Time To Go To Bed* Two Actors, Vocal Quartet, and Chamber Ensemble	1978
Earl Kim	*Dialogue* Piano and Orchestra	1959
Leon Kirchner	*Lily* Opera after Saul Bellow's *Henderson the Rain King*	1977
Oliver Knussen	*Flute Concerto* (work in progress)	—
Ellis Kohs	*Symphony No. 2* Chorus and Orchestra	1957
Barbara Kolb	*Trobar Clus* Chamber Ensemble	1970
	"Yet That Things Go Round" Chamber Ensemble	1987
Ernst Krenek	*The Bell Tower* Chamber Opera in One Act	1957
	Sestina Voice and Instrumental Ensemble	1958
	Quaestio Temporis Chamber Orchestra	1960
Matthias Kriesberg	*Parte Sin Novedad* Soprano and Five Instruments	1985
Paul Lansky	*Values of Time* Woodwind Quartet, String Quartet, and Tape	1987
Thomas Oboe Lee	*The Cockscomb* Soprano, Trumpet, Violin, Bass, Piano, and Percussion (two players)	1981
Douglas Leedy	*Usable Music II in Bb* Chamber Ensemble	1966
John Anthony Lennon	*Seven Translations* Soprano, Clarinet, Violin, and Piano	1988

Fred Lerdahl	*Chromorhythmos* Orchestra	1972
Jeffrey Levine	*Chamber Setting No. II* Chamber Ensemble	1967
Gerald Levinson	*Light Dances, Stones Sing* Chamber Orchestra	1978
Peter Lieberson	*Concerto for Four Groups of Instruments* Chamber Ensemble	1973
Robert Lombardo	*Quintet for Winds*	1958
Alvin Lucier	*Serenade for Thirteen Winds and Pure Wave* *Oscillators* (first version)	1985
Steve Mackey	*Journey to Ixtlan* Chorus and Orchestra	1986
Thomas McKinley	*Premises and Expositions* Chamber Orchestra	1968
	Quadruplum Soprano, Flute, Violin, Piano, Chorus, and Chamber Ensemble	1971
Bruno Maderna	*Giardino Religioso* Chamber Orchestra	1972
Ingram Marshall	*String Quartet* Amplified String Quartet and Live Electronic Sound	1985
Michael Martin	Composition	c.1965
Donald Martino	*Concerto for Wind Quintet*	1964
Bohuslav Martinu	*Incantations, Piano Concerto No. 4*	1956
Salvatore Martirano	*Underworld* Four Actors, Four Percussion, Two Double Basses, Tenor Sax, and Tape	1965
Walter Mays	*Islands* Chamber Orchestra	1981
Joyce Mekeel	*Serena* Mezzo-soprano, Speaker, and Chamber Ensemble	1975
Jan Meyerowitz	*Esther* Opera in Three Acts	1957
Stephen Mosko	*Superluminal Connections I: The Atu of Tahuti* Orchestra	1985

Lawrence Moss	*Scenes* Small Orchestra	1963
Frederic Myrow	*Music for Orchestra*	1965
David Myska	*Excursion* Orchestra	1985
Robert Newell	*Concerto* Piano and Chamber Orchestra	1964
Eugene O'Brien	*Mysteries of the Horizon* Chamber Ensemble	1987
Betty Olivero	*Presenza* Chamber Ensemble	1986
Julian Orban	*Himnus ad Galli Cantum* Soprano and Chamber Ensemble	1956
Harry Partch	*The Bewitched* Dance Satire for Dancers and Instruments	1957
Oedoen Partos	*Concerto* Violin and Orchestra	1965
Stephen Paulus	*Letters for the Times* Chamber Chorus and Chamber Orchestra	1980
John MacIvor Perkins	*Music for Thirteen Players*	1964
George Perle	*Concertino for Chamber Orchestra*	1979
Burrill Philips	*The Return of Odysseus* Chorus, Orchestra, and Baritone Soloist	1957
Mel Powell	work in progress	—
Shulamit Ran	*Ensembles for Seventeen* Chamber Ensemble	1975
Bernard Rands	*Suite No. 2: Le Tambourin* Orchestra	1986
J.K. Randall	*Mudgett* Pre-recorded Female Voice and Converted Digital Tape	1965
David Reck	*Number Two* Actress, Flute, Bass Clarinet, Percussion, Guitar, Violin, and Bass	1965
Steve Reich	*New York Counterpoint* Clarinet and Tape	1985

Jay Reise	*Paraphonia* Chamber Orchestra	1978
Roger Reynolds	*Blind Men* Three Trumpets, Three Trombones, Tuba, Percussion, Piano, and Chorus	1966
Philip Rhodes	*Autumn Setting* Soprano and String Quartet	1969
Wallingford Riegger	*Symphony No. 4*	1957
Dennis Riley	*Concertino* Trumpet, Cello, Piano, Harp, and Percussion (2)	1976
George Rochberg	*Music for Magic Theater* Chamber Ensemble	1965
Loren Rush	*Nexus 16* Chamber Ensemble	1964
R. Murray Schafer	*Gita* Three Trumpets, Two French Horns, Three Trombones, Tuba, and Chorus	1967
Gunther Schuller	*String Quartet No. 1*	1957
	Music for Chamber Ensemble	1972
Joseph Schwantner	*Wind, Willow, Whisper* Chamber Ensemble	1980
Robert Selig	*Chocorua, A Music Theatre Work* Chamber Ensemble and Voices	1972
Roger Sessions	*Concertino* Chamber Ensemble	1972
Ralph Shapey	*Dimensions* Soprano and Twenty-Three Instruments	1960
	Songs of Ecstasy Soprano, Piano, Percussion, and Tape	1967
	String Quartet No. 7	1972
Seymour Shifrin	*Satires of Circumstance* Mezzo-soprano and Chamber Ensemble	1964
Shelia Silver	*Canto* Baritone and Chamber Ensemble	1979
Faye-Ellen Silverman	*Passing Fancies* Chamber Ensemble	1985

Stanley Silverman	*Elephant Steps* Opera in One Act	1968
	Choruses from the Midsummer Night's *Dream Show* Chorus and Sixteen Musicians	1971
Leland Smith	*Quintet* Bassoon and Strings	1956
Harvey Sollberger	*Chamber Variations* Twelve Players	1964
Claudio Spies	*Tempi* Fourteen Instruments	1962
Rand Steiger	work in progress for chamber ensemble	—
Halsey Stevens	*Septet* Two Violas, Two Cellos, Clarinet, Horn, and Bassoon	1957
Alan Stout	*Nattstycken* Alto, Speaker, and Chamber Ensemble	1970
Tison Street	*String Quintet*	1974
Morton Subotnick	*The Key To Songs: A Tone Poem in Collage* *After a Surrealistic Novel* Two Pianos, Percussion, Viola, Cello, and Live Computer Sounds	1985
Ira Taxin	*Fanfares and Dialogues*	1976
James Tenney	*String Quartet*	1984
Hectar Tosar	*Aves Errantes* Chamber Ensemble	1959
Joan Tower	*Flute Concerto* (work in progress)	—
Preston Trombley	*Chamber Concerto* Piano and Chamber Orchestra	1975
Richard Trythall	*Continuums* Orchestra	1968
Ben Weber	*Serenade for Strings*	1956
Henry Weinberg	*Cantus Commemorabilis*	1966
Louis Weingarden	*Seven Poems of Constantine Cavafy* Narrator and Chamber Ensemble	1971
Richard Wernick	*Cadenzas and Variations* Viola and Piano	1970
	Contemplations of The Tenth Muse Soprano and Piano	1976

Olly Wilson	*Voices*	1970
	Orchestra	
David Winkler	*Concerto for Piano and*	1974
	Twelve Instruments	
Stefan Wolpe	*Piece for Piano and Sixteen Instruments*	1962
Maurice Wright	*Stellae*	1978
	Orchestra and Electronic Sounds	
Charles Wuorinen	*Chamber Concerto*	1964
	Flute and Ten Players	
	Concerto for Amplified Violin and Orchestra	1972
Jurg Wyttenbach	*Encore*	1970
	Chamber Ensemble and Electronic Tape	
Ramon Zupko	*Life Dances*	1981
	Orchestra	

APPENDIX, 1987–1988
(Works commissioned in the months after Paul Fromm's death)

John Cage	*One Hundred and One* (work in progress) (commissioned jointly with the Boston Symphony Orchestra)	—
Elliott Carter	*Remembrance* (In Memoriam Paul Fromm) (commissioned jointly with the Boston Symphony Orchestra)	1988
Todd Macover	work in progress	—
Carolyn Steinberg	work in progress	—